The War Within
Our HEARTS

"Our Lord! Accept from us (this act);
indeed You are the All-Hearing, the All-Knowing." (2:127)

To our parents and teachers:
those who brought us from the heavens to this Earth,
and those who will help take us from this Earth to Heaven.

The War Within Our HEARTS

Habeeb Quadri and Sa'ad Quadri

With an introduction by
Imam Zaid Shakir

KUBE
PUBLISHING

First published in England by Kube Publishing Ltd,
Markfield Conference Centre
Ratby Lane, Markfield,
Leicestershire LE67 9SY
United Kingdom
Tel: +44 (0) 1530 249230
Fax: +44 (0) 1530 249656
Website: www.kubepublishing.com
Email: info@kubepublishing.com

Originally published as *The War Within Our Hearts*,
High Quality Educational Consulting, 2008.

Cataloguing-in-Publication Details are available from the British Library

ISBN 978-1-84774-012-0 *paperback*

Cover design and typesetting by Nasir Cadir
Initial cover design concept by Rizwan Ahmed (contact: riz160@yahoo.co.uk)

Contents

Part II: Solutions

Introduction
The War within our Hearts

Verily, they were youth who believed in their Lord and we increased them in guidance. And we strengthened their hearts when they took a stand, saying: "Our Lord is the Lord of the Heavens and the Earth; we will never call on any God besides Him. If we do so we would have uttered a grave enormity". (Qur'an 18:13-14)

One of the disheartening features of our modern, or, for some, our postmodern condition, is that it encourages us to live lives of isolation, oftentimes divorced from even the crowds that might surround us in our bustling cities. We have friends and acquaintances, but many times these relationships do little other than disguise our fundamental state of alienation. One of the disastrous consequences of our state is sometimes we become isolated from even our true selves and from our Lord. This condition of alienation from Allah is reinforced and encouraged by many of the messages that permeate our environment. Those messages are conveyed via television, movies, popular music, literature, and many other means.

Many of the techniques currently used to convey those messages were unknown to many Muslim parents who have migrated to the West from towns or villages in the Muslim world: places that lacked in some instances electricity, not to mention televisions, iPods, the internet, and related media. For those Muslim parents who converted to Islam here in the West, those techniques, some of which are designed

– by way of example – to create lifelong brand identification in six-month-old babies, were in rudimentary and simplistic stages of development during their youth. Now, they are fully perfected and along with other forces that currently influence and help to shape the psychic and spiritual environment we are developing in, they create an atmosphere that challenges a believer in ways that are unprecedented in human history.

Through various forms of print and electronic media we are encouraged to consume things we do not need, to have a lifestyle that threatens our planet and erodes our humanity. We are encouraged to fornicate and to abandon the values, mores, customs and conventions that have supported family life since the advent of humans on this planet. We are encouraged to use drugs, drink alcohol, and to become gluttons by consuming ever expanding quantities of food "products". We are encouraged to interact with the opposite gender in ways that are debasing and potentially destructive. How can a young Muslim negotiate such rough terrain? Answers to this question have been scarce, especially answers that resonate with our youth. Now, Habeeb and Sa'ad Quadri, youth organizers, experienced teachers, and perhaps more importantly, people who have walked down the challenging, obstacle-strewn road many of our youth currently travel, provide a meaningful answer. That answer lies in this book, *The War Within Our Hearts*, an insightful volume that takes on many of the issues confronting Muslim youth here in the West, sometimes with humor, oftentimes with brutal frankness, but always with sound knowledge and great clarity.

The War Within Our Hearts, focuses the attention of the reader on the real battleground where the war for the soul of our youth is being waged, the hearts. If we are looking for the source of the problems that are currently vexing Muslims, young and old alike, there could not be a better starting place, for our Prophet ﷺ has reminded us: "Surely, in the body there is an organ, if it is sound the entire body is sound and if it is corrupt, the entire body is corrupt. Verily, it is the heart." (Bukhari, 52; Muslim, 1599)

It has been said that the enemies that are waging a relentless war against our hearts are four: the ego, Satan, our whimsical desires, and the world itself. The most dangerous of these enemies is the ego. The soul in its unrefined, unconstrained, immature state is the ego. That it is the more dangerous than even Satan is illustrated by the fact that, during Ramadan, Satan and his dupes are chained up. The Prophet ﷺ mentioned, "When Ramadan arrives the gates of Paradise are flung open, the gates of Hell are slammed shut, and the Satans are shackled." (Bukhari, 1898, 1899; Muslim, 1079) However, there are people who engage in the most egregious sins during Ramadan. How could this be when Satan and his dupes are shackled? We are taught that those sins emanate from the ego.

We mentioned that one of the characteristics of the ego is its spiritual immaturity. Its maturation takes place over time. This fact is illustrated by the story of Joseph in the Qur'an. When the soul of the wife of the Aziz of Egypt, Zulaikha, was immature and unrefined, she was a prisoner of her passions and impulses. As a result, she could not see the blame that she bore for her attempt to seduce Joseph. To prove her lack of guilt she gathered the women of her circle and had Joseph enter the room. When they lost control of themselves in his presence, she used that as an affirmation of her innocence. However, as the years passed and her soul matured, she was able to free herself from her passions, to see her guilt as well as the negative impact her actions had in the events leading to the wrongful incarceration of Joseph. She declared: *I do not absolve myself of any blame. Surely, the ego commands what is vile, except for those my Lord has mercy on. Indeed, my Lord is Forgiving, Merciful.* (Qur'an 12:53)

This verse emphasizes something of tremendous relevance for our youth. Specifically, the ego naturally inclines towards vileness. Hence, without a conscious effort to restrain it and to nurture it towards maturity, it will naturally draw a person towards the vileness and vulgarity that is intricately part of contemporary youth culture: the alcohol, drugs, violence, abusive language, misogynistic attitudes, pornography, crass music, sloppy dress, rejection of parental authority, and other vices that stand in clear contradistinction to sound Islamic principles and teachings. The immaturity of the soul is one of the main reasons why many of the things mentioned here are particularly attractive to young people nowadays. These are some of the very issues that Habeeb and Sa'ad Quadri deal with in this enlightening volume.

As for Satan, his enmity towards the human being is clear. Allah mentions in the Qur'an, *Verily, Satan is an enemy unto you, take him as an enemy.* (Qur'an 35:6) For his part, Satan mentions, *Because you have waylaid me, I will lie in ambush of them on your straight path. I will assault them from their front, their rear, their right and their left. And you will not find most of them thankful.* (Qur'an 7:16-17) It is said that the assault of Satan from these various vantage points means that he will assail us in our worldly affairs, our religious life, and cause us to doubt the veracity of the Hereafter. We often forget that Satan has declared war on us and is waging that war on many fronts. We live our lives as if his assault is fictitious or harmless. If we are to survive his attack we have to be constantly on guard against his guiles and conspiracies.

Given that Satan is at war with us, we must fight back. Allah encourages us in the Qur'an, *Therefore, fight you altogether the dupes of Satan. Surely the scheme of Satan is weak.* (Qur'an 4:76) To implement this order, do we sit back and allow Satan to bring the battle to us? If we do so we will inevitably be overwhelmed. We have to go on the offensive. We go on the offensive against Satan by staying in a constant state of purity, by means of *wudu'* and *ghusl*. We stay on the offensive with the frequent remembrance of Allah. We stay on the offensive by regularly reciting the Book of Allah. We also fight Satan and his dupes by avoiding the arrogant and self-centered attitude that led to his demise.

Satan's arrogance was instrumental in his being prevented from entering Paradise. Allah mentions in the Qur'an, *And when We said to the Angels bow down before Adam, they did so, except Iblis, he refused, arrogated himself, and was among those who reject faith.* (Qur'an 2:34) As for those who will inhabit the heavenly home, Allah describes them in the following terms, *This is the Home of the Hereafter that We have made for those who do not desire to exalt themselves on Earth, nor to work corruption therein; and the* [good] *end will be for the God-conscious.* (Qur'an 28:83) Satan fell from Allah's grace owing to his arrogance. Many believers will be saved due to their humility. Each and every one of us has to choose which of these two paths we will follow: the path of arrogance or the path of humility.

Controlling ones whimsical desires is also instrumental in holding on to one's religion and successfully living a life of faith. Falling victim to our whims is very similar to the way some of us succumb to the whispering of Satan, for it is during our moments of heedlessness that we become susceptible to both. However, resisting our soul's whimsical desires is not an easy matter. In addition to mental and spiritual alertness, we have to consciously struggle against those whims. Allah says in the Qur'an, *As for one who fears when he will stand before his Lord, and denies his soul its whimsical desires, surely Paradise will be his refuge.* (Qur'an 79: 40-41)

This is the "jihad" that Habeeb and Sa'ad Quadri are alluding to in the pages of this book. That is to say the "jihad" to control of tongue, the "jihad" to turn away from the pornographic pictures and the lewd, indecent lyrics. The "jihad" to resist the temptation to attend the wild parties, or to dress in a manner totally unbecoming a Muslim. The practical solutions Habeeb and Sa'ad Quadri offer to these and many other issues currently vexing our youth are tactical steps in the "Greater Jihad". Allah mentions in the Qur'an, *As for those struggling for Our Sake, we will guide them to Our Paths. Indeed, Allah is with those possessing inner excellence.* (Qur'an 29: 69) Those paths are the paths leading to Allah. They are only accessible to those who struggle for His sake. Habeeb and Sa'ad Quadri have rendered our youth an immeasurable service by delineating for them very practical and easily performed steps to guide that struggle.

Finally, the world itself is a great enemy of the human being. However, this is not necessarily so, for the world can also be a source of great benefit. Whether the world is an enemy or a source of benefit lies in how a person approaches it. If one approaches it with caution and the understanding that it has many potential pitfalls, then one can negotiate past its hazards and traps. The Prophet ﷺ mentioned that "The world is a source of beneficial enjoyment, and the most beneficial thing in it is a righteous spouse." (Muslim, 1467) This *hadith* clearly presents us with a clear message concerning the potential benefit of the world. However, the Messenger of Allah ﷺ also said, "The world is sweet, green [and lush]." (Muslim, 2742) This seemingly innocuous statement is a warning against the seductive temptation of the world. It can definitely benefit us, but it can also seduce us.

Its seductiveness lies in its ability to blind us and lead us to believe that its delights are unsurpassed and that they endure. When a person has been seduced by the world, he comes to believe that there is nothing nicer and more pleasurable. He believes that he is in a paradise, and he believes that the delights of the world are permanent. The believer knows better. The Prophet ﷺ described this state of delusion in a few brief words when he mentioned, "The world is a paradise for the disbeliever and a prison for the believer." (Muslim, 2957) This is a powerful statement concerning the nature of the world. The disbeliever is deluded into believing there is nothing more pleasurable than this world, and his entire life devolves in a reckless, hedonistic endeavor. As for the believer, he lives like a prisoner, realizing that like an incarcerated person, he cannot do what he wants, when he wants, how he wants. However, like a prisoner he looks for opportunities to do things that will benefit him when he returns home.

A thoughtful prisoner will take advantage of the educational and vocational opportunities that are available for him. He will take advantage of the free time to read abundantly, expanding his mind and raising his consciousness, as was the case of Malcolm X and countless others. He will also hit the weights and work himself into tip-top shape. Hence, the Prophet ﷺ has presented an amazing parable for the world. In it the believer is constrained by the rules put in place by the warden. However, he takes full advantage of the opportunities he has, even in such a harsh and dangerous environment, of those things that will benefit him when he goes before the parole board and when he finally returns home.

With this invaluable book, Habeeb and Sa'ad Quadri have reminded our youth of these realities. They have shown us many of the weapons that the ego, Satan, our whimsical desires, and the world use in their war against our hearts, and have given tremendous insight into the means of defence that we have at our disposal to resist the combined assault of those forces. They do this in a readable and accessible fashion that will not repulse those youth that have been pushed away from religion by the strict formalism and rigid thinking of scholars and teachers who, through no fault of their own, are simply unfamiliar with the mentality of Western Muslim youths and the severity of the challenges that they face just to be Muslims. Hence, when they remind us of the war that is being waged on the battleground of our hearts, they do not cause us to despair. Rather, they encourage us by letting us know that this is a winnable war. Armed with that knowledge, let us all enter into the fray and begin fighting back.

Imam Zaid Shakir
March 31st 2009
Berkeley, California

Preface
How to Read this Book

Living in a world in which image is everything, people strive to mould themselves into other than they are. Understanding this, we realized when writing this book how we may be constructing a false image of ourselves, causing people to see us in a light we do not deserve. Henceforth, it is important we make it clear that neither of us are scholars. We are simply your Muslim brothers struggling to gain Allah's pleasure and attain Paradise.

Furthermore, it is important to note our goal is not to lecture or put anyone down – we know anyone who reads this book is probably better than us. Our guiding purpose has always been to define and help deter us from certain struggles that we as Muslim youth in America will certainly face. Though we may feel these struggles are unique, we are often unaware that many of our young brothers and sisters share the same struggles. Just as soldiers look to their fellow soldiers for aid and assistance as they face the enemy on a battlefield, as Muslim youth we must band together and help one another in our daily combat against *Shaytan* (Satan) and our *nafs* (inner self). The mere recognition of our shared struggle can help strengthen our brotherhood and sisterhood, which in turn may help shield us from the hellfire.

Shaytan, rejected as he is, refuses to enter hell alone. Rather, he wants to mislead others, pulling them away from Allah ﷻ in this world and toward hellfire in the hereafter. After Satan was expelled from heaven, he sought reprieve from Allah ﷻ. When he was given reprieve, he declared that he would work to lead astray Allah's servants.

He (Allah) *said: "Then go from here! It is not for you to show pride here, so leave! Verily you are from those who are disgraced." He* (Shaytan) *said: "Give me reprieve until the day when they are resurrected!" He* (Allah) *said: "Verily you are from those given reprieve." He* (Shaytan) *said: "Now, because You have sent me astray, verily I shall ambush them from the straight path. Then I shall come upon them from in front of them and from behind them and from their right side and from their left side, and You will not find most of them as being thankful."* (7:17)

In a fit of arrogance, Satan let slip his plan of attack against the believers, namely that he wants them to no longer be grateful for the various bounties bestowed upon them by Allah ﷻ. The easiest way for Satan to do this is to target, pollute, and destroy the place where gratefulness is born, the heart.

Shaytan regularly targets our hearts, knowing it is most valuable and vulnerable to our existence. This is made very clear in the Qur'an as Allah ﷻ mentions, *The day wealth and children will not benefit* [a person]*, except those who return to Allah with a sound heart.* (26:88-89) Success and failure on the Day of Judgment lie in the state of our heart. The Prophet ﷺ has mentioned the key role of the heart in our lives, "And indeed there is an organ in the body, if it is sound, the body will be sound, and if it is corrupt, the body will be corrupt. Verily it is the heart." (*Hadith*) This same heart will be the key to a person's heaven, or the path to a person's hell. Thus, the war within our hearts is possibly the greatest battle that a person will ever fight. In this book, we hope to shed some light on pertinent topics through both our own experiences, and our experiences when working with others in order to help you make the right decisions on the proverbial battlefield.

Before jumping into the book, we feel it is important to understand the text is divided into two equally relevant parts. In

Part I, the chapters address problems we regularly face, followed by practical solutions on how to overcome these challenges. Part II includes long-term goals and solutions we should strive to implement in our lives in order to better them in this *dunya* (this world) and in the *akhirah* (hereafter).

While reading and upon completion of this text, we suggest the following:

- Beware of Shaytan's deception.
- Self-reflect by recognizing some of our own weaknesses.
- Ascertain ways to improve the condition of our heart.
- Implement some of the practical solutions through both action and commitment.

Also, the way this book is structured is that we will use Arabic terms interchangeably with their English equivalent. When a term is first used in Arabic, we will italicize that term and follow it immediately with its definition in parenthesis. Also, you will find the following also present after the following words in English (there may be a slight difference for the dual or plural form):

- Allah ﷻ – Glory be to Him and He is Most-High
- Prophet Muhammad ﷺ – May Allah's prayers and peace upon him
- Any other prophet ﷿ – Upon him be peace
- Male Companion ⦿ – May Allah be pleased with him
- Female Companion ⦿ – May Allah be pleased with her
- Male Scholar/Righteous individual ⦿ – May Allah's mercy be upon him
- Female Scholar/Righteous individual ⦿ – May Allah's mercy be upon her

All verses cited have the citation of the chapter and verse from which they were taken. Any *Ahadith* (Prophetic traditions) will be cited simply with the word *Hadith* (Prophetic tradition) in parenthesis. The reason for this is that we have used common ahadith that have been reported as being authentic or sound. If anyone wishes to know where any particular Hadith may be found, these can be found in the standard Hadith collections.

Finally, each chapter is intended to be independent of all other chapters. So a chapter may refer to another chapter in the book, but comprehension of any chapter is not dependent upon reading any other chapter. We ask you to begin, as Muslims should begin all things, with the name of Allah ﷻ.

Part 1: **Problems**

Who Knows You Better?
Introduction

As society grows increasingly self-sufficient, we as human beings often feel that nobody knows us better than ourselves. After all, we are more conscious of our own thoughts, intentions, and actions than anyone else. Consequently, many of us feel there is no one better to advise us than ourselves. Yet, what we fail to remember is that Allah ﷻ is our Creator. He created us, and having created us, He knows what is best for us. For example, the Daimler-Chrysler Company is known for making many cars, in particular, the Mercedes Benz. Being the manufacturer, Daimler-Chrysler would naturally know the best way to care for a Mercedes. When customers purchase a Mercedes they are given an owner's manual to follow. That manual highlights all aspects of the car's care: from what type of gas should be put in the car, when to get an oil change, what the car's tire pressure should be, and so on and so forth. In that same light, Allah ﷻ created us knowing what is best for us. If our goal is to please Allah ﷻ, then the best way to please Him would be by to follow the manuals He has given us, specifically the Qur'an (the word of Allah ﷻ and the Holy Book of Islam) and the *Sunnah* (the Prophetic example) of the Prophet Muhammad ﷺ.

Our minds and bodies work with capacities that are at times beyond our awareness. There are certain innate physical strengths and weaknesses that have been bestowed upon us. Those strengths and weaknesses are at times obvious – for example, a human being cannot pick up a car. At the same time, an example of our strength is that we have been blessed with the intellect to have created machinery that can lift cars for us. Like the physical body, the spiritual side of a person also has strengths and weaknesses. Allah ﷻ, our Creator, is aware of all humanity's strengths and weaknesses. The story of Prophet Adam ﷺ gives us a great reminder of how foolish and weak creation can be without the help of Allah ﷻ.

When humanity was created, Allah ﷻ displayed its superiority over all of Allah's creation through the display of Prophet Adam's knowledge. Thereafter all the angels were ordered to bow down to Adam ﷺ.

So the angels prostrated, all of them together. Except for Iblis; he refused to be amongst those who prostrated. (Qur'an 14:30-31)

They all subsequently bowed down to him, except *Iblis* (the formal name given to the Devil once he rejected the command of Allah ﷻ), who refused to bow down to Adam ﷺ. Thus humanity's torments and tests began.

Lessons from Adam and Iblis

Lessons

Before the creation of man, there was a community of *jinn* (a being made from smokeless fire that, along with mankind, is also responsible for its actions) that Allah 🌺 had created. A group from this community became excessively disobedient to the extent that Allah 🌺 ordered the angels to destroy them. The angels subsequently destroyed all of the *jinnat* (plural of jinn) but spared the life of an infant jinn named Azazil (who later becomes Iblis), thinking that this young child could not do any harm. When they returned to Allah 🌺 they explained to Him what had transpired. Allah 🌺 told them that He knew what they do not know.

Azazil was raised by the angels and, as a result, grew to be a very righteous and knowledgeable servant. In fact, Azazil quickly became the most knowledgeable of jinn as he saw the angels and the Bounties of Allah 🌺. Thus, through his experience and presence in the heavens, Azazil was able to raise himself above the angels in piety and knowledge. But when Allah 🌺 told him to bow down to Adam 🌺, Azazil allowed that knowledge to deceive him and he became arrogant. Consequently, he disobeyed Allah 🌺.

> *And* (remember) *when We said to the angels: "Prostrate yourselves before Adam." And they prostrated except Iblis (Satan), (who) refused and was proud and was one of the disbelievers.* (Qur'an 2:34)

He thought himself better than Adam ﷺ and in his own mind convinced himself that he did not need to prostrate to Adam ﷺ because he was created from fire while Adam ﷺ was created from clay.

He (Allah) said: "What prevented you (O Iblis) that you did not prostrate yourself, when I commanded you?" Iblis said: "I am better than him (Adam), You created me from fire, and him You created from clay." (Qur'an 7:12)

It is important to reflect on this because many of us unknowingly use this mode of thinking when we make a mistake. Rather than accepting we have made a mistake, we begin to rationalize our actions and accept them as being correct.

In contrast, if we look at our father, Prophet Adam ﷺ, and his story in heaven, we learn a lesson that may forever benefit us in our lives. When Prophet Adam and his wife Hawa ﷺ were in heaven, they were told to enjoy everything that their hearts desired and were commanded only to stay away from one thing.

O Adam! Dwell, you and your wife, in Heaven and eat (enjoy) from it from whatever you wish, but do not come near to this tree, lest you be amongst the wrongdoers.
(Qur'an 7:19)

When imagining this amazing scene two things need to be considered – who was involved and where this took place. Here was the first prophet and his wife, and they had the opportunity to be in heaven. Let's say that again, *heaven!* They saw and could enjoy everything in paradise. The only thing they were to refrain from was going near a tree. But Iblis was very cunning and he eventually led them to the tree. They ate its fruit, so causing them to lose out on the heavenly bounties given to them.

Think about the item they were tempted by, a fruit; they were tempted by a fruit and they lost heaven because of it. Today we are tempted by much more than a fruit. It shows us that Shaytan will always try his best to confuse and misguide all of us, no matter what his tool is. He wants us to feel alone when presented with temptations, so falling victim to our desires. We should never forget what goes on in our minds and hearts is not just something we are going through individually; rather, the majority of the time many, if not all, of us are having the same thoughts. Remember, Shaytan wants to lead us all astray, and not just some of us.

Returning back to the story, when looking at Shaytan, his immediate reaction was to be upset with Allah ﷻ for his mistake. In fact, not only was Shaytan upset with Allah ﷻ, but he also blamed Allah ﷻ for his own mistake.

He (Shaytan) said: "Now, because You have sent me astray, verily I shall ambush them from the straight path." (Qur'an 7:16)

Imagine the nerve of Shaytan, blaming Allah ﷻ for *his own* sin! This act of blaming and despairing of the mercy of Allah ﷻ was what sealed Shaytan's fate as cursed.

When Adam and Hawa ﷺ ate from the tree, they took the exact opposite route. Rather than blaming Allah ﷻ, they realized the mistake they made by eating fruit from the tree and immediately cried out to Allah ﷻ:

They said: "Our Lord, we have wronged ourselves! If You do not forgive us and have mercy on us, we shall certainly be of the losers." (7:23)

Without delay Adam and Hawa ﷺ recognized their mistake, took responsibility for it, and repented to Allah ﷻ for their mistake. We must relate to their example by understanding there are areas in which all of us make mistakes; many of them are quite common. However, rather than making excuses or even legitimizing our sins, it is better to recognize our mistakes and try to move on from there.

There are numerous Ahadith that describe the Day of Judgment. From these Ahadith, some clearly show that certain individuals will be forgiven for their sins, despite the fact that the magnitude of their sins – both in quantity and quality – made them appear as people of the hellfire. When examining these particular Ahadith more closely, we see that a common factor in many of them is that those who accepted their mistakes and repented were forgiven by Allah ﷻ. This, as a principle, isn't foreign to us.

Throughout the world, criminals often admit to their crimes in return for a lighter punishment. Simply by admission, they are spared a harsher fate. We are without doubt guilty of many crimes against Allah ﷻ. It is very important for us not to justify these transgressions; rather we need to admit them in front of Allah ﷻ in this world and beg for His forgiveness. We are by our very nature weak; He does not expect perfection from us.

Allah wants to make your burden light for you, for man was created weak. (4:28)

Thus, when we do sin against Him, it is important to return back to Him sincerely.

"Every child of Adam is a sinner, but the best from amongst the sinners are those who repent." (Hadith)

This is exactly what our parents Adam and Hawa ﷺ did in heaven, and this repentance is what distinguishes the result of their mistake from the sin of Iblis.

Finally, many of us assume that when we commit sins that we will repent later on and redeem ourselves, for Allah ﷻ is the Most-Merciful. This is the logic *shayatin* (devils) use. They sin and misguide others, assuming they will invoke Allah's mercy before this world ends – foolishly trying to outsmart Allah ﷻ. Such people only hurt themselves. Remember, every sin comes with a price, and if Allah ﷻ is merciful to us, we will see our errors in this life and repent for them, with ultimate disgust and remorse for our actions.

Allah accepts the repentance of those who do evil in ignorance and repent soon afterwards. (Qur'an 4:17)

However, if we are arrogant or delay our repentance, we never know when we will die. This is the mistake of the Pharaoh, who was shown the signs of Allah ﷻ through the Prophet Musa ﷺ, but he was in love with his worldly status and power and faced a horrible death. It is said that as the Pharaoh was drowning, he wanted to repent to Allah ﷻ. The angels, being afraid that even after all of his transgressions Allah ﷻ would still forgive the Pharaoh, began to put dirt into his mouth to make him drown faster.

Until he was about to drown, he said, "I believe that there is no god but the One in whom the children of Isra'il believe, and I am among those who submit." [Allah replied] *"Is it now (that you come to believe) while you were rebellious before and you were amongst those who caused mischief."* (Qur'an 10:90-91)

Allah ﷻ did not accept his repentance and preserved his body as a reminder to all of humanity.

So today We shall save your body so that you may become a sign for those who come after you. (Qur'an 10:93)

Those who do not repent before they die will undergo a horrific judgement in the hereafter, and they will be the only ones to blame at that point. If Allah ﷻ chooses not to shower His mercy upon us then we will suffer an indescribable torment in the akhirah.

Are My Intentions Alright?
Intentions

If you look through many books of Hadith, the first Hadith the compiler often uses is the Hadith on intention: "Verily, actions are (rewarded) by intentions."

As a side note, when a compiler of Hadith begins to write his book, the compiler is not writing a new book. Rather, he is compiling a book of Ahadith he has selected from the treasury of the statements of the Prophet ﷺ. So when the author places a Hadith in the beginning of the compilation, it is done intentionally to deliver a specific message and lesson to both the author and the reader. Many authors place this specific Hadith, out of the many Ahadith that exist, at the beginning of their compilations, to show the importance of this Hadith and the message it relays – the basis of everything we do must have the proper intention.

The Prophet ﷺ reminded us that all actions are by intentions. Some scholars have analyzed this Hadith and have come to the conclusion that without the correct intention an action cannot even exist! But putting this technical discussion aside, the main point to note is that intentions are essential to our daily lives. Sometimes we do an action, and although that action may seem pure, our intentions end up spoiling it. At the same time, we may be involved in an action that may seem mundane, but with the proper intention that action becomes an act of worship.

In essence, when we look at an act of worship, that act is not too different from any other action in our lives. For example, when Sa'ad used to cut weight (a term wrestlers use to indicate losing large amounts of weight) before a meet, he would often not eat the preceding day. The act of not eating for a day does not carry any reward on its own. But, if Sa'ad were to make an intention to fast that particular day, then the entire day of not eating becomes worship. Another example of intentions, and one that we may be able to relate to more, is that of going to school.

As students, we spend a large amount of our day in the classroom or studying for classes. We often spend over ten hours of our day related to school work. As a result, we complain about being unable to focus more on our religious growth. What if we could change all those hours spent studying and in class to worship? Obviously we would all be interested, and the solution is simple. If when we wake up, we tell ourselves in our heart we are going to school in order to please Allah ﷻ through gaining knowledge to benefit the *din* (religion) – be it through teaching that knowledge, getting a job through that knowledge and serving the din, earning money with that job and knowledge to spend on the din (which includes providing a *halal* (lawful) income for the family) – then those hours are no longer just "for school," but are now for the sake of pleasing Allah ﷻ. Hence these actions become worship. In the same manner, we can also spoil our intentions.

When we turn our actions away from being solely for the sake of Allah ﷻ, we spoil our intentions. The most common example of this is our prayer. There is a famous story of a young man who was praying in the *masjid* (mosque) when two individuals walked in. Upon seeing this young man praying with *khushu'* (intense focus and concentration), they began to comment about how pious this man must be, complimenting him and his prayer. The young man, realizing this, prolonged his prayer and began to perfect it even more, which drew even more compliments. Upon completing his prayer, the young man turned to the men and told them that he was also fasting. The prayer and the fast were no longer being performed with the proper intention, to please Allah ﷻ, but were now being done to receive praise from the men. This story, though humorous, highlights an important example of how easily an intention can go awry and no longer remain solely for pleasing Allah ﷻ. On the flip side, Allah ﷻ is so merciful that He is quick to forgive and reward a changed intention.

As mentioned by Shaykh Yassin Roushdy in his book, *The Heart, The Tongue, Their Sicknesses and Cures*:

> There are four stages that a person goes through before committing a sin. The first stage is when the idea crosses your mind – and most of the time Shaytan insinuates this idea. You are not held accountable for this stage. In the second stage you feel the desire to do the action. For example, a person is fasting and while he is walking in the street he smells a certain kind of food that he loves and automatically feels the pangs of hunger and the desire to eat. This is a feeling which you cannot control and hence you are not punished for it. During the third stage you become inclined to commit the sin. In the fourth stage you intend to commit the sin – you have made up your mind. At this stage you are judged by Allah ﷻ as the Prophet ﷺ explained: "Actions are only judged according to intentions."

It is always good to check our hearts when we are doing anything. At many times we know in our hearts when we are doing something wrong. When reading about the prophets ﷺ and the great Muslims of the past it is amazing to note how much time they took in reflection, soul-searching in order to pinpoint even the most miniscule of negative actions and thoughts – they were always self-improving and maintaining their piety in the process.

This is very important, especially when we are young and building a foundation for how we practice the din. Iblis does not like this, so if he knows we are following the commandment of Allah ﷻ, he will try to persuade us to change our intentions. For example, we might go to the masjid for prayer and notice people there saying, "*masha'Allah* (literally, what Allah wills), you have come to the masjid for prayer, if only other kids would be like you." After such comments, if we begin coming to the masjid hoping that people will compliment us again, we have cheated ourselves of the opportunity to be rewarded by Allah ﷻ for this action.

This example should inspire us to check if our intentions are pure. If, when we do something such as help out at the masjid or give a talk, we find ourselves waiting for someone to say something to us or waiting around for someone to recognize us doing that good action, then we know our intention is impure. If, even before we do a good act, we are already thinking about what people would say or which people will see us then, again, our intention needs to be put into check. Shaytan will always try to confuse us. The best thing for us to do before conducting a good action is to take a few seconds and supplicate to Allah ﷻ, asking for purity of intention so that our good actions will be accepted and our mistakes can be forgiven.

In a *hadith qudsi* (a Hadith in which the Prophet ﷺ relates, in his own words, a statement of Allah ﷻ) the Prophet ﷺ told a story about what will happen to three individuals – a scholar, a wealthy man, and a martyr – on the Day of Judgment. The scholar will be called forth for questioning and will be reminded of the favors that were bestowed upon him. He will be asked what he did with those favors. The scholar will respond by saying he gained knowledge in order to propagate the din and teach people for the sake of Allah ﷻ. Allah ﷻ will tell him that he has lied and that his intention was for people to call him a knowledgeable man, and he was called a knowledgeable man. Thus, he received the reward of his intention in this world and will be thrown into the hellfire.

The second individual to be called forward will be a man of wealth. He will be reminded of the various blessings that were bestowed upon him and will then be asked what he did with his wealth. The man will respond by saying he donated his money for the sake of Allah ﷻ. Allah ﷻ will tell this man that he has lied and that his intention was for people to call him a generous man, and he was called a generous man. Thus, he received the reward of his intention in this world and will be thrown into the hellfire.

The final individual who will be called forward will be a martyr. He will be reminded of the various blessings that were bestowed upon him and will be asked what he did with these blessings. The man will respond by saying he fought in the battlefield for the sake of Allah ﷻ and made the ultimate sacrifice, giving his life up for the din. Allah ﷻ will tell this man that he has lied and that his intention was for people to call him a brave man, and after his death he was called a brave man. Thus, he received the reward of his intention in this world and will be thrown into the hellfire.

This Hadith highlights the importance of keeping our intentions purely for the sake of Allah ﷻ. Here we had three individuals who did great actions, but their intentions were impure. As a result, they may have done what seemed to be extremely righteous deeds, but they did not achieve the ultimate goal – the pleasure of Allah ﷻ. We should remember this story and try to keep ourselves from falling into the same fate.

PRACTICAL SOLUTIONS

- Before any action, especially worship, make your intentions clear to yourself and purify them.
- After completing any action, ask Allah ﷻ to accept your actions.
- Before doing anything, search your heart for the reason you are doing the task: is it for fame, to show off, etc?
- Turn a mundane action into worship by rectifying your intention, thereby connecting the action to Allah ﷻ.
- Remember, Allah ﷻ will reward you for even thinking about doing a good action.

The Mirage Box
TV

Today's youth are flooded with various pop culture images and trends within society. As a result, our identities are vulnerable. As we grow we begin to lose our original identity as it becomes replaced with what is accepted as mainstream. Thus, a child who would otherwise not be interested in a certain lifestyle will quickly begin to adopt that lifestyle in order to be accepted by society. After all, in our time, common role models tend to be celebrities and stars; it is their faces that are plastered everywhere. It is a sociological truth that the environment plays a large role in shaping an individual. Therefore we must surround ourselves with people and operate in areas that are best suited to the development of our din – we must remember that the continually emulated pop culture of today is not filled with the best role models. Television is a breeding ground for the type of lowly behaviour we should do our best to avoid following.

Ever since its invention, the popularity of TV has skyrocketed. Once it was rare to find a home with a television, now it is rare to find a home without one. Initially it seemed this new invention would be a means for people to relax and enjoy themselves, taking entertainment from the auditory world into the visual world. Soon businesses and corporations began to notice the extreme influence television had on the world. Not only were people deriving information from television, but they were soon using it as a means of relaxation and entertainment, escaping the stresses of the world. Television soon became the choice drug of the masses, intoxicating them from reality. Families soon began spending time together in front of the television, unknowingly absorbing the dangerous rays that beamed from this mystical box. Even more unknown to them was that they were absorbing a new way of life through the television and losing themselves in the process. Family time, what used to be an opportunity to spend quality time with each other, is now spent like zombies in front of the television. In 2008, every person watched an average of over 26 hours of TV each week in the UK, with an average of 42 ads every day; in the US, people watched an average of over 35 hours every week. On top of that, watching video online or through our phones is becoming more popular too, while the amount of television viewing is not decreasing.

The advertisers of the soft drink "Sprite" were smart when they coined the tagline, "Image is everything". This simple phrase perfectly describes our society where everything is about image and perception – or how we are perceived. This is why stars like David Beckham, Michael Jordan, Jennifer Lopez, Eminem, and Brittany Spears get paid millions of dollars for endorsing everything from clothes to cars. Television offers corporations a vast selling platform. The money is not in the show, it's in the commercials and product endorsements. Businesses pay millions of dollars for 30-second time slots to sell their products. After all, they know consumers watch a lot of television and that during the commercial break, most individuals will continue watching as they wait for their programme. These few seconds may seem trivial, but businesses know these are valuable moments in which they can penetrate the minds of individuals they hope will digest their messages. Furthermore, companies pay big money to have their products displayed within television shows as well. We've all noticed popular clothing and food brands displayed within scenes of popular television shows – actors and actresses interact with these products, lending their popularity to further the allure of the item. These images are subsequently stored in our minds. The cash corporations that pay to have their logos or products placed just in the background of a movie know that this is money well-spent as these images will be imbedded in hearts and minds of their viewers.

When we were younger, Habeeb wanted to have a wristband on his arm and a knee brace on his knee because Michael Jordan wore them; this was the case despite the fact that he had no problem with his knee. He merely wore the brace because he wanted to be "Like Mike". Yes, while there is no problem with that on the surface, in reality we unknowingly begin to look to celebrities for guidance in other areas of our lives. Perhaps wearing a headband or knee brace when playing basketball might not seem like a problem, but there are individuals who become completely obsessed with stars and begin to copy everything from their dress to the way they act. It is difficult to completely emulate our favorite celebrities if we only copy one part of their lives. Thus, people begin to venture in deeper and deeper until they have taken upon themselves a lifestyle that is completely un-Islamic. It began innocently enough by wearing a jersey or certain shoes, but it soon grew to something much more overwhelming. The worst part is that when we copy someone from our society, we deny ourselves the wonderful opportunity of following the greatest person to ever walk this Earth: the Prophet Muhammad ﷺ (this will be discussed in another chapter).

Well, that stuff may be obvious and you're probably now wondering "what's actually wrong with TV?" OK, fair enough. We should start with the more obvious factors and move to those that are more subtle. Any individual watching television regularly over the past several years can testify that the content has become increasingly worse. Many scenes allowed on programmes today would never have been shown a few short years ago. Now there is a general acceptance of nudity and scenes with adult content on television. Dressing provocatively in public is widely accepted as normal. This desensitization and tolerance of inappropriately dressed men and women is truly a tragedy. Even if families do not allow such content to be viewed in their households, while parents are at work kids will gravitate to cable television which is basically an open invitation for such material to be viewed by our youth.

Needless to say, such content is obviously *haram* (unlawful). Islam requires all men to cover from their navel to their knees (including both the navel and the knees), while it requires women to only expose, at most, their hands, face, and feet. If such is the case, then what justification can we give to watching any programme that shows the opposite gender inappropriately dressed? Allah ﷻ says in the Qur'an to the believing men and women to lower their gaze and guard their modesty.

> *Say to the believing men that they should lower their gaze and guard their modesty.* (24:30)

> *Say to the believing women that they should lower their gaze and guard their modesty, and they should not display their ornaments except what appears of them.* (24:31)

This action specifically requires all people of one gender to divert their gaze when another gender is present (this will be discussed in another chapter). That is, a person may look at someone of the opposite gender for the amount of time it takes to identify who the person is and thereafter to divert one's gaze. If that person cannot be identified or if we do not know that person, then we should lower our gaze once we recognize the person's gender. Thus, a person is not permitted to constantly stare at a person of the opposite gender in order to fulfill their desires or for any other reason. This standard also proves true in conversations between distant relatives and non-relatives of the opposite gender. So, if this is the case, then how can we justify watching television?

So that we can understand the actions of the characters presented, we are required to watch the television show. If the visual aspect was not present then it would merely be a radio programme. Television programmes, which are firstly a visual form of media, are produced to keep a person visually engaged. As a result, many programmes largely feature attractive people because producers and directors realize the audience would much rather look at people who are pleasing to the eye. Therefore most actors and actresses look like models. We must ask ourselves a serious question: "Does any part of me want to watch this show because I like the appearance of a particular character?" If so, that programme is causing us to sin – which does *not* mean, however, that if we are unattracted to the person on the TV that it becomes permissible.

Without a doubt, it is much more difficult to lower our gaze when seeing someone attractive compared to someone who is unattractive. Furthermore, the Qur'anic injunction does not specify believers to lower their gaze around those who are attractive; rather, it gives a general statement to lower our gaze around anyone of the opposite gender. Lowering the gaze, though a difficult task, is one of the strongest tools that a person can use to attain heaven.

The eyes are a vital part of our body. They play the often overlooked role of the window to our hearts. The eye acts as a camera, capturing countless images and storing them in our hearts. In fact, anything we see, hear, or taste will directly affect our hearts. That is why it is extremely important to keep all of our sensory input morally pure. The heart acts as our hard drive, processing any information entering it. If a computer's input is affected by a virus, the hard drive will suffer and the computer will not be able to work properly. In that same regard, if our input is corrupted, our heart will be negatively affected, and our bodies and souls cannot reach their full potential.

To make another comparison, a cell or mobile phone cannot function without its SIM card. The phone may be completely intact or even new, but without its SIM card it can never retrieve the signals sent by the service tower or mast. If our hearts (the SIM card in this example) are impure and unable to accept Allah's signal (sevice tower/mast), then no matter how many features the phone (our body) has, it will be absolutely useless.

There are many harms associated with not guarding our gaze, most of which we will discuss later in Chapter 6,

"Lowering Your Gaze". Among these harms is that our hearts will be blackened by constant sinning.

Verily on their hearts there is rust from what they used to do. (Qur'an 83:14)

We need to realize that this darkness of the heart can, in some cases will, cause the heart to eventually become sealed.

Allah put a seal over their hearts and on their hearing, and on their sight is a veil. (Qur'an 2:7)

This seal prevents guidance and the light of Allah ﷻ from entering into the heart. The Prophet ﷺ told his companions that the heart rusts like iron, and the means of polishing this rust is by reading the Qur'an and remembering death. To polish and clean the heart prepares it for Allah's guidance and allows light to enter it.

Allah is the light of the Heavens and the Earth. (Qur'an 24:35)

There is a story of a famous scholar, Imam Shafi'i ﷺ, who was gifted with an amazing memory. During his studies, he noticed a deficiency in his memory and immediately reported it to his teacher, Waki' ﷺ. His teacher asked him to think deeply as to whether or not he may have done something incorrect that would cause his memory to be affected. After much thought he realized that when walking he had recently seen the heel of a woman. By maintaining that glance, his memory had been affected. When he told his teacher about this, his teacher told him to repent immediately, which he did, and his memory was restored. Imam Shafi'i ﷺ actually recorded this incident and the advice of his teacher in a poem:

*I complained to [my teacher] Waki' about the weakness of
    my memory,
So he advised me to abandon sin.
And he informed me that knowledge is a light,
And the light of Allah is not given to a sinner.*

Imagine how potent a misdirected glance can be if it caused the memory of Imam Shafi'i 🕮 to weaken! This story may seem a bit strange because we regularly see much more than the heel of the opposite gender and do not see any type of negative affect in our lives. To understand this story better, we should consider the following.

When people buy a new car, especially if it is expensive, they act differently than they did with their previous car. If they park in a parking lot or car park, they may park away from other cars to avoid being hit accidentally by a careless driver or an errant grocery cart or shopping trolley. If they are driving and they reach a gravel road, they may decide to take an alternate route or drive very slowly over the gravel road. Sometimes they will walk around their cars to see if there are any new scratches. If they do have a new scratch or dent on their cars, it will greatly bother them and they want to get it repaired right away. In a new car, anyone can notice even the smallest scratch, dent or scrape.

But for a person who is driving an old car with many scratches and dents, a new scratch or dent often goes unnoticed, both by the driver and others. Even if the dent is noticed, a person may overlook it and not get it repaired because it would be useless to fix one dent while the others around it have gone untouched. On the other hand, the owner of a new car will painstakingly examine and have even the smallest scratch repaired, because even slight damage takes away from the perfection of that car.

This is the situation with our souls. We have beaten up our souls by sinning to such an extent that a new sin does not seem to have any effect on us. The reality is that each and every sin has such deep and grave effects that we would weep if we noticed them. But, if for example we are already looking at things that are haram, eating things that are haram, or missing *fajr* (pre-dawn) prayer as a result, then we won't notice the affect of any new sin on us just like a new dent or scratch won't be noticed on a beat-up old car. But the righteous people, like Imam Shafi'i ﷺ, were so concerned to preserve their souls that they would immediately notice the grave effect the smallest mistake had on them. The *Sahabah* (companions of the Prophet ﷺ) would notice if on any given night they did not wake up for *tahajjud* (a voluntary prayer best offered in the last third of the night). Furthermore, since they were so careful about abstaining from sins, if they did commit a sin they noticed its effect, for example, a loss in memory or not waking up for tahajjud, and would immediately recognize their sin, repent for their sin, and remove it from their lives. But if people commit hundreds of sins on a daily basis, how will they ever be able to decide which one has which effect?

Abstain from sin, be it open or secret. (Qur'an 6:120)

Thus, when we commit a sin, we should immediately repent and ask Allah ﷻ to not only forgive us for that sin, but also to remove the effects of that sin from our lives.

As human beings, our eyes can wander constantly and look at whatever they desire yet still we are never satisfied. A famous scholar from the Indo-Pak subcontinent Maulana Ashraf Ali Thanwi ﷺ mentions that when people first become involved in misdirecting their gaze these actions act like sparks. Soon after, a hunger grows in the hearts of these people and they are never satiated by their subsequent glances: each glance causes their hunger to grow. As the hunger grows, the attempts to satisfy that hunger also grow.

What eventually happens is that when people enter into marriage and meet the first person they should have an intimate relationship with, they feel disappointed with their new spouse as they have many images of the opposite gender lodged in their memory and they begin comparing. Rather than their spouse being the first person whom they have ever fully seen, they have a backlog of beautiful images of other people stored in their hearts from years of gazing upon the opposite gender. As a result, people begin to think about how such an actor has nicer eyes than their spouse, or how such an actress has nicer hair than their spouse. The artificially made-up television faces and fabricated TV personalities become reasons to be hyper-critical of their own spouses. When spouses are constantly disappointed in one another because their expectations of the marriage or of each other have become so distorted by aligning their anticipations with unrealistic ideals, then marriages may ultimately fail.

The ideals portrayed on television are a reflection of our society. As society digresses, so does what is portrayed on television. Sexualized vocabulary and images have become widespread in the media. The danger is that what Islam abhors has become more acceptable because of the mainstream portrayal of sexualized themes on television, which are subsequently reflected in our lives. Additionally, Muslims no longer see anything wrong with swearing or cursing, pre-marital interaction, violence, partying, and whatever else the media flaunts because we, as viewers, get lulled into acceptance of these actions, ultimately taking up such behaviours ourselves.

The discussion about television is not restricted only to whether it is halal or haram. Many prominent commentators have noted its potentially detrimental effects. In his book, *Four Arguments for the Elimination of Television*, Jerry Mander argues that television has the potential to cause great harm to our communities through the fact that its messages are relayed by a minority, elite group, and are transmitted to the masses. As a result, our moral compass is determined by the opinions of only a few people. When this occurs, the vast majority of people are led to believe that a certain ideal is correct, despite the fact that that certain ideal is based on their personal opinions. This unwittingly places everyone under a type of overexposure to an elite consensus, which has been called "manufacturing consent". Elite agendas are manifestly spread through the use of television. After all, as Mander, and others like Neil Postman argue, television is a medium that is editorially determined by the broadcasters wherein the viewer excercises choice, but only within the context of the programming given. We may control what we watch by having a remote control in our hands, but the messaging follows certain common themes and reflects a certain elite consensus despite the apparent choice in programming.

Furthermore, Mander also argues that watching television, being in essence a passive action, puts the viewer into a passive state. The constant signals that are absorbed by the viewer lead to a pacifying of the active mind. The mind, being inactive, accepts the images and dialogue and stores them away. These thoughts may become ingrained in our minds, eventually being adopted as our own thoughts and attitudes, often without adequate self-reflection. This passive learning has swamped us with the teachings and views of others and often made us take them on as our own. In *Amusing Ourselves to Death*, Postman also argues that television is used for entertainment and susbsequently makes everything into entertainment. Things that were sacred and important have now become integrated with entertainment. We see clearly that even sitcoms that air social problems in a family or relationship are all solved within a half hour time slot. It has led many of the students at our schools, for instance, to hold the false expectation that problems are not a big deal because everything will have a happy ending within a short period of time. When this unfounded "reality" collapses, so does the resolve of many of our youth. Many panic and become depressed over situations and conditions they are experiencing in life.

In the end, however, there is some benefit in television, if used with discretion. For instance, there are educational programmes that we can benefit from. Various shows on the Discovery Channel or other nature shows can allow us to grow closer to Allah ﷻ by recognizing the greatness of His creation. At the same time, we have to make sure that we are not fooling ourselves into thinking that by drowning ourselves in educative programming that we will grow closer to Allah ﷻ. Unwinding and relaxing is a part of life, but excess in anything is not from the path of those who are successful.

PRACTICAL SOLUTIONS

- Offer *du'a* (supplication/prayer) to Allah ﷻ that He protects your gaze.
- Offer du'a by reciting Allah's beautiful names like al-Muhaymin (The Protector) so that He may protect you from watching things that are not good for you. You can use al-Barr (the Righteous) when asking that He make you a righteous human being.
- Limit the hours of television and movies that you watch.
- Exchange television time for reading or playing sport.
- If and when you do watch television, watch with family members and not alone.
- Do not have a television or computer in a bedroom, but have it in a room that is accessible to everyone.

In Da Club
Parties

The time of high school and college or secondary school and university gives way to a new daily schedule, and, more often than not, a new night schedule as well. Many of us will be minding our own business when handed a flier or asked to go to a party. We have all thought about going to a party, and some of us did go – often regretting the decision later on. Others were fortunate enough to have Muslims around who cared enough to provide an Islamic outlet. In general, the main reason why most of us would go to a party is simply out of curiosity. We want to see what will happen and experience what all the talk is about. In Islam, there is a very established principle in which we cut actions off at the root. This is why Prophet Adam and Hawa ﷺ were ordered:

> *And do not go* (you two) *near to this tree, or you will be amongst those who wrong themselves.* (Qur'an 2:35)

Adam and Hawa ﷺ were ordered not to eat the fruit of the tree; Allah ﷻ knew that just by their coming close to the tree they would be tempted to eat its fruit. Thus, He commanded them both not to come near it. As human beings we are naturally curious and are likely to transgress if put in a tempting environment.

Allah ﷻ reveals much in the Qur'an regarding human nature relating to gender intermingling. When speaking about people He does not say "do not commit *zina*" (pre- or extra-marital sexual relations); rather, He says:

And do not come close to zina, for indeed it is an indecent thing and an evil way. (Qur'an 17:32)

The same principle applies here. Allah ﷻ knows that human beings will naturally be attracted to each other, so He commands humanity not to come close to fornication and to stay away from the environment of sin.

Simply put, any bad environment can destroy us. Regarding clubs, initially the curiosity will be just to see it. Shaytan will tell us to just go and see how the party is so that we can tell others how bad it was. Let us quickly consider how the mind works. A person will first think, "I'll go to the party to check it out, but I won't dance." Then the thought comes, "If I do dance, I'll just sit and move to the beat. And, if I sit, it will just be with people of the same gender." Then, the thought arises to get up and dance, but "I'll just dance on my own." However, dancing on your own looks foolish so the person will decide to dance with someone of the opposite gender but with no brushing against each other. But contact is part of dancing, so maybe there will be some of that, but definitely no kissing. But where there is mutual attraction, there may be a kiss, but of course it won't go any further than that. And, obviously, "After I've been to a party once, I'll never go again." There will be people who only go and sit, but not dance or do anything else. But no one can say that the thought of going a few steps further never comes up. The path to hell is paved with good intentions that went bad in the heat of the moment.

Let us think about it another way. Why do most people go to clubs? If it is merely to listen to music, then a person can listen to music on the radio. If it is to dance, then a person can dance at home. The vast majority of people go to meet new people, particularly of the opposite gender. That is why clubs will give promotions like "Ladies Night", where it is free admission to women – to set the environment for people to meet others. On "Ladies Night", men are sure to attend as they know there will be more women because of discounted or free admission. The stage is now set to do something wrong and it is that very same environment that influences us and can lead to our committing sin. If everyone around us is doing something haram that comes naturally to them, then slowly we too will let our guard down. If we are at a party or club and someone attractive approaches us and wants to talk, or asks us to dance, what will we say? "Sorry, I came as a spectator...just to watch" – like the club is a tennis match. Even our friends may encourage us to mingle with the opposite gender – they might even help us out with a pick-up line or two.

Clubbing is a culture: by Thursday and Friday people start getting ready for these parties. If we take part, we cannot go in regular clothes so we dress up in a cool way. Also, our group of friends becomes the types that hang out in such places. Imagine, taking the *imam* (religious leader) of the mosque to a club. No one would do it! Why? Simply put, the imam is not the person who any of us would want put in an environment that is un-Islamic. Even the most modest of people would eventually get used to that environment. Maybe the first time we would be nervous, but we can become more and more comfortable each time we go thereafter. It is like learning to swim. The first time we may just stick our feet in the water, but eventually we can plunge into it completely, drawn in by our surroundings.

Finally, we are very good at fooling ourselves. Some excuses that we make are so convincing that even though we are making them up, we end up believing ourselves. Of all these excuses made the most common is fooling ourselves into believing that we may commit a sin now, but we will stop after committing this sin. We may attend a party with the intention to go just once and not go again. This excuse actually comes in the story of Prophet Yusuf ﷺ where his brothers plotted to kill him. They were jealous of the attention that he received from their father, Prophet Yaqub ﷺ, and wanted to get rid of him.

> *Kill Yusuf or throw him in some far away land so that his father's face* [attention] *may be your's alone.* (Qur'an 12:9)

Thereafter, they justified their actions by saying:

> *And after that you may become a righteous group.* (12:9)

The brothers thought they could commit this final sin and then become righteous, but this is the trap of Shaytan. He wants us to think that we can commit our sins one final time, and then thereafter we will be righteous. But the problem is that every sin opens the door to the next sin, which is why the Prophet ﷺ advised us to follow a sin with a good deed. This will help stop us from committing another sin. If not, then the next time the chance to sin arises, we will tell ourselves that we'll do it this last time and never again. After throwing the Prophet Yusuf عليه السلام into the well, his brothers had to cover up their sin by lying to their father, which was yet another sin. Each sin that they committed had to be covered up by a subsequent one. This is the nature of sin: a sinful act rarely if ever stands alone.

The next time we decide that we'll do that sin once more and then we'll never do it again, think of how the brothers of Prophet Yusuf عليه السلام thought the same thing. Eventually they became caught up in the web of sins their own hands had spun and did not get out of it until they were exposed to their father and their brother by Allah ﷻ. The last thing we want for ourselves is to get caught up in the web of our sins, only to be found exposed, stuck on its sticky strands.

PRACTICAL SOLUTIONS

- Hang out with good friends who will help you make good decisions.
- Reduce time spent watching music videos or shows glamorizing party life.
- Do not go to events/parties that have music and dancing – don't tempt yourself.
- Pray to Allah ﷻ that He helps you make right decisions and surrounds you with good friends. Use these names of Allah ﷻ to start your du'a: al-Muhaymin (the Protector) for Allah ﷻ to protect you from temptation, and al-Qawi (the Strong) for Allah ﷻ to make your *iman* (faith) strong.

6

Who Dat?
Lowering Your Gaze

There is no doubt that lowering the gaze is tough. When we are walking and we see someone we think is attractive, somehow the phrase "who dat?" comes flying into our minds. As one of the five senses, sight is a killer, especially in a society obsessed with looking good and attracting others. When society makes short skirts, halter tops, muscle shirts, and other similar clothing fashionable, it is not so people can feel comfortable in these clothes. This is purely about parading beauty and sexuality. Aside from clothing, people are increasingly having cosmetic surgery to enhance their figures and become more attractive. Even perfumes are being made with pheromones that have been found by scientists to attract the opposite gender. Just look at the names of some of these perfumes: "Allure", "Passion", "Obsession" etc.: they are designed exclusively to attract other people.

What is funny is when we think, "Man, that girl is *hot!*" or "He is *fine!*", we take that feeling of attraction and justify to ourselves why we had to look at that person – it was impossible not to feel that way. Or, we think we will just take one look and after that not look again. In reality, this is how Shaytan works. Human nature dictates that we will never be satisfied. The Prophet ﷺ was very clear when he said: "Nothing will satiate the son of Adam except the dirt of his grave." (Hadith)

Although this refers specifically to wealth, it is relevant to other areas of our life. It is just like a car: when we look at it for the first time we think that is the one we want, but, one year later, a better car comes out and we want that instead. The same holds true of looking at someone attractive for the first time, for example, in a college lecture hall – we say to ourselves, "Wow, who is that?" But by the end of the semester we might think someone else is better looking. We simply do not know when to stop. This is when Shaytan whispers, "Hey, I am only looking. What else can a person do? Am I supposed to just look at the floor or the sidewalk all the time?" What we fail to realize is that Shaytan wants us to take that first step – he knows that once we have that first taste we may not be able to control ourselves.

There is a famous story mentioned in Hadith about a righteous and pious worshipper from the Bani Isra'il by the name of Barsisa. Barsisa lived alone, spending his days and nights in the worship of Allah ﷻ. One day, three brothers who wanted to go out on *jihad* (meaning "struggle", and in this context it refers to fighting in the cause of Allah ﷻ) needed to find someone to watch over their sister whom they could not leave behind alone. They asked Barsisa if he would be willing to care for her. Being a righteous servant, Barsisa naturally said no deeming it wrong to watch over a woman not related to him and without a close male relative present. However, when the brothers left, Shaytan began to whisper to him that he should in fact care for their sister because the brothers would likely find someone else to do so, and that other individual would not be as righteous as he and would take advantage of her. Barsisa approached the brothers and agreed to care for their sister provided that he could do so without interacting with her.

Initially, Barsisa would make food for the sister and leave it outside his door, not venturing close to her home. A short time thereafter, Shaytan whispered to him that it is unbefitting for a woman to walk in public, compromising her modesty, just to be able to eat. Barsisa, thinking this his own idea, decided to take the food and leave it outside her door. A short period of time passed before Shaytan then suggested it was very demeaning to have her fetch her food like an animal: it would be better for Barsisa to greet her from outside and ask how she was doing, and then leave the food for her. This lasted for some time before Shaytan whispered it to him that it was very strange that he yelled from one side of the door while she yelled from the other.

Shaytan prompted Barsisa to think that as he was the most righteous person in his community – he could enter her home and sit on the other side of the room to give her company. It would not be anything inappropriate, and she must be lonely without her brothers. Barsisa began to do this and slowly Shaytan enticed him closer to sin. Eventually, Barsisa and the sister had pre-marital relations, and she became pregnant. Barsisa knew her brothers would return and began to worry. Shaytan whispered to him that he should murder her and the child and bury them inside her home. After all, Barsisa needed to keep his reputation for being a righteous man and would repent for his sins. Thus, Barsisa carried out this plan and killed the sister and her child, burying them in her home and covering up the grave.

Eventually, the brothers returned from jihad and approached Barsisa regarding their sister. Barsisa, blatantly lying, told them their sister had become ill and had eventually passed away due to her illness. He had created a fake grave in the city and directed the brothers there. The brothers went to the grave and mourned their sister, carrying out the rites for the deceased. One night, while the brothers slept, Shaytan came to each of them in their dreams explaining what had transpired between Barsisa and their sister. Upon waking, one brother told the other two that he had a strange dream and described it to them. Both brothers were astonished as they too had the exact same dream. They went to the grave of their sister and dug it up, finding it was indeed a fake grave. Then, as the dream indicated, they went to their sister's home and unearthed the bodies of their sister and her child.

The brothers immediately rushed to Barsisa and took him forcibly to the king to be executed for his crimes. Being extremely worried, Barsisa became desperate to be saved from his dilemma. Shaytan then appeared to Barsisa and told him that he could help him on one condition; Barsisa had to make *sajdah* (prostration) to Shaytan. Barsisa agreed, and when he bowed down to Shaytan, Shaytan left him. Thus Barsisa, once the most righteous worshippers of his time, died bowing down to Shaytan.

This story is a great example of how one small sin, when justified and accepted as being harmless, can lead a person astray. Temptation overpowered even the most righteous worshipper of the time. In reflecting on this story we should not feel hopelessness, but rather we should realize Allah ﷻ has given us the knowledge to escape this end by heeding the various warnings He has given us.

Allah ﷻ tells believing men and women how to protect themselves from the effects of a misdirected glance and how to navigate the safest route with respect to being modest with one another:

> *Say to the believing men that they should lower their gaze and guard their modesty.* (24:30)

> *Say to the believing women that they should lower their gaze and guard their modesty, and they should not display their ornaments except what appears of them.* (24:31)

A beautiful aspect that was expounded upon by scholars regarding the end of this particular verse.

> *And Allah is aware of what you do.* (24:30)

In the verses of the Qur'an that address the transgressions people commit, Allah ﷻ ends these verses by proclaiming His mercy and His forgiveness. Yet, at the end of the verse on lowering the gaze and guarding one's chastity, Allah ﷻ affirms that indeed He knows what we do. Imagine, every time we misdirect our glance, Allah ﷻ sees what we do and witnesses our accompanying thoughts. Sadly our hearts have blackened to the extent that knowing Allah's displeasure of this act neither affects nor deters us from it.

If we find this is the case, we should try to think of the following, "Would I misdirect my gaze if my parents were watching me?" Now, imagine if one of our teachers were watching us. Next, imagine if a righteous person or a *sahabi* (a companion of the Prophet) were watching us. Lastly, think how we would feel if the Prophet ﷺ were watching us as we committed this transgression. If any of these situations would cause us to want to lower our gaze, then the larger question to ponder is, "Why am I embarrassed to commit sins in front of other human beings but not Allah ﷻ when He is watching me at all times?"

While the greatest tragedy lies in having gained Allah's displeasure, we are also unable to realize how each stolen glance or seemingly innocent interaction we allow ourselves causes serious damage to our life in this world. Whenever we find a person attractive or good looking, and then interact with that person – though it may be completely innocent – what ultimately happens is that those interactions become ingrained in our subconscious. That is why at night, before we go to sleep, thoughts of that individual and our interactions with that individual will go through our minds.

Eventually we may no longer think about that person, be he or she an actor, celebrity or just a person in our lives. However, when we are finally blessed with the opportunity to marry, after the honeymoon phase we may begin to notice our spouse's imperfections. Shaytan will remind us of the thoughts ingrained in our subconscious from all the pre-marital interactions we had to run wild in our minds and we may then begin to dwell on our spouses' deficiencies. It is just as bad that we will compare our spouses with the models, actors, and actresses we were infatuated with in the past. As we have allowed our eyes to wander and store images just as a digital camera stores images when it takes a picture, we will be faced with the huge challenge of comparing our spouses with those who are made "perfect" through airbrushing, starvation, plastic surgery, and all the other man-made ways humans try to present themselves as other than they truly are.

The reality is that we will find ourselves in situations working with the opposite gender. Many of us are involved with our local masjid or other Muslim or charitable organizations. Furthermore, our schools and workplace will also require us to interact with the opposite gender. During this time, we should try to keep a few principles in mind. First off, we should make sure that we are honest with ourselves about our intentions. In the cases of work, school, and Islamic work, our hearts should always know what the reason and purpose of our conversations are. If the thought arises in our minds of impressing whom we're speaking with or trying to do more than the necessary task at hand, then maybe our interaction may go down the wrong road.

Also, we have to be very clear about where we are speaking to one another. If our conversations are taking place in the classroom in the presence of the teacher, there is more of a chance it will stick to business. However, if we decide to meet for coffee at a local café to discuss the assignment in English class or the plans for the next masjid dinner, then Shaytan may easily change our intention. Furthermore, we have to be very mindful of what we talk about. Small talk has its place, time, and recipients. Do not indulge in small talk when unnecessary. This is not to say that we should be rude. It is understood that we should greet one another and be cordial. However, we should be conscious not to speak about unnecessary items. This is where Shaytan will make us think that since we were having that important conversation about the relief dinner that everything is OK: this is where many of us make our mistakes.

Finally, we have to abstain from speaking at night-time. There is no reason why a brother should have to call or see a sister, classmate, or co-worker at midnight in an informal setting. Many times we think to ourselves that this is for the sake of Allah ﷻ, but is it really? Would Allah ﷻ really like us to speak like this at this time of night, when our hearts and minds incline towards romance? We have to be smart and honest with ourselves.

When speaking to one another, we should maintain a necessary degree of modesty. While the Qur'an has ordered us to lower our gaze, but sometimes it becomes unclear as to how we can do this at school, work, or the various other daily situations we encounter. If we need practical guidance on this issue, it is best to consult with our local scholars for further advice.

Many of us are afraid that we will upset the person whom we are speaking with. But would we rather please that person and upset Allah ﷻ instead? Allah ﷻ has advised the Sahabah about their interactions in the Qur'an. All of us can agree that the Sahabah were greater than us. Allah ﷻ repeatedly says in the Qur'an that He is pleased with them. Some of them were given the glad tidings of entering Jannah before they passed away. Furthermore, the Prophet's wives – the *Ummahat al-Mu'minin* (the mothers of the believers) – were told,

> **O wives of the Prophet! You are not like other women.** (Qur'an 33:32)

Their status has been raised in this life and in the hereafter. Yet, when Allah ﷻ addressed them He was very clear that if they had to speak to an unrelated male out of necessity they should do so in a certain way.

> **Do not be soft in speech.** (Qur'an 33:32)

Many times we find ourselves changing our tone of voice in order to attract, even if unconsciously, the opposite gender. Brothers and sisters in faith may both, consciously or unconsciously, speak in softer tones to each other. And these softer voices may eventually become flirtatious. Allah ﷻ was referring to the best of women in conversation with the best of men. There is no follower of the Prophet ﷺ that is greater than his Sahabah. So when the *Ummahat al-Mu'minin* are speaking to them, Allah ﷻ ordered them not to be soft in their speech because,

> **Lest he in whose heart there is a disease may be moved by desire.** (Qur'an 33:32)

If Allah ﷻ is warning the best group of men and women about the potential harm in their interaction, then who are we to say that our intentions are always clean and our hearts may not have a disease in it. This is why we have to be very straightforward with ourselves and others. The command may have been directly at that time for the Sahabah, but it is even more so directed towards all the believers today.

Furthermore, Allah ﷻ also has commanded the Sahabah if they needed to ask the Prophet's wives for anything.

And when you ask them for anything you want, ask from behind a barrier. (Qur'an 33:53)

Again, this command is directed towards the best followers of the Prophet ﷺ. It is because they implemented the commands of Allah ﷻ that He was pleased with them. Thus, if we are unsegregated, then we should at the very least act modestly and avert our gaze. Generally speaking, when out in public space, we should always seek to keep the company of a mature and Godfearing friend, for it will encourage us to act with modesty and decorum. Although taking these measures may sound harsh in today's climate, Allah ﷻ gives us the reason as to why we should do this:

That is purer for your hearts and for their hearts. (Qur'an 33:53)

If the war that we are fighting is in our hearts, and success belongs to the one with a pure and sound heart on the Day of Judgment, then we should try to follow these steps in order that our hearts remain pure.

Furthermore, there are many ways that we can interact with the opposite gender while still looking normal. We don't have to turn our backs to the person when we're speaking or send social signals that are rude and impolite. Guard your gaze with confidence and good manners, and not with an attitude of disgust or a judgemental frame of mind. Do not make the person feel like an alien, but be confident in the virtue of modest conduct you are trying to live by. In the end, we cast our gaze aside out of respect for the other person: we value him or her as a person, and we do not seek to reduce that other person to a mere object of sexual desire. As we mentioned in the chapter on TV, when a society is captivated by one ideal, then it will naturally come to think that this is the only way. In the early 1900s in America, men would not generally gaze at women on the street. It was natural for them to lower their gaze. Books like *The Beauty Myth* and *A Return to Modesty* highlight that this way of life was once common and natural. However, once various media became dominant in our culture, we have changed without realizing it.

In the end, we are accountable for everything that we do. On the Day of Judgment, even our very own body parts will bear witness for or against us, bearing witness to the way we used them. We need to ask ourselves, 'How will we want our eyes to testify?'

PRACTICAL SOLUTIONS

- Surround yourselves with people who influence you to be modest and guard your gaze.
- Fast for a few days at a time to reduce sexual desire.
- Remember that Allah ﷻ is watching you.
- Guard your gaze when talking to the opposite gender.
- Limit interaction and avoid unnecessary talk with the opposite gender.
- Pray to Allah ﷻ that He help you in controlling the nafs and desires.
- Limit watching TV, especially dramas and music videos.
- Check your heart and ask why you are looking at people.
- Ask Allah ﷻ to help you only see things that benefit you and to protect your gaze from things that harm you.
- When speaking with someone of the opposite gender we should make sure to:
  - Act modestly
  - Keep our intentions pure
  - Speak only about what is necessary
  - Speak at an appropriate time and place

Double Trouble
Drinking & Drugs

Two of the most destructive elements in our society are alcohol and drugs. Crime, theft, rape, murder, and many other tragedies have often been caused by these two vices. Even in clubs alcohol is used so people can lose control and do things they might not have done if they were sober. The results, however, can be devastating. Date rapes often occur because people were drunk and they took advantage of the situation. Drugs are just as prevalent in clubs, illegally distributed so people can enjoy themselves more. Alcohol, tobacco and illegal drugs are vast global businesses. The illegal drug trade around the world is over $320 billion dollars a year; global trade in alcoholic drinks is $64 billion a year, and for tobacco $28 billion. The United States, for example, has the largest drug market with a street value of $35 billion dollars in 2000, although the costs to society like medical care, crime, welfare costs and lost work time came to $168 billion dollars. In the UK, the illegal drug market was £4-6.6 billion (around $7-12 billion dollars) in 2004. In the UK there are over 100,000 smoking-related, 7,000 alcohol-related and 2,500 drug-related deaths every year.

We might think we will never be involved in drugs, but all the 19.9 million illicit drug addicts in America in 2007 (8% of the population) and the 7 million in Britain in 2004 (12% of the population) were once young and when their mothers asked them what they wanted to be when they grew up they would never have answered, "a drug addict". They just thought –

like we do – that they would control themselves. But with substances that manipulate our mental state, keeping control is not always as easy as people make it seem. There is a reason why drug dealers always give drugs away for free the first time around – they know that once a person takes that first step and experiences that drug high, that person might become a life-long customer. The dealer has a new money-maker.

Take cigarettes for example. Even though countless advertisements tell us one out of three people will die from smoking, there are still 3,000 people who start smoking everyday! There are even warning labels on the cigarette cartons themselves! This is the Iblis-syndrome: "I know better than anyone else." Remember, Iblis was ordered by Allah ﷻ to bow down, but he refused to bow down thinking he knew better than everyone else. As a result, what bliss was guaranteed for him was destroyed by his own hands.

If these temptations were not difficult enough, all of these things – smoking, drinking, and drugs – gain an appeal through peer pressure; if the environment is such, we might be tempted or asked to participate. Many people who never thought they would smoke admit to starting because they were constantly surrounded by those who smoked. Remember, the path to participation is that of small steps. A UK government study in 2006 found that "smoking, drinking and drug use are all highly related behaviours". A US government report in 2009 showed that "illicit drug use [was] concurrent with alcohol use (i.e., during or within two hours of last alcohol use)". Rarely do we find people who go directly to the strongest drugs. When addicts are unable to reach their initial high through the same drug, they may look for a bigger high with another drug.

Then there is society's drug of choice, which most do not even recognize as a drug. Alcohol is the most widely used drug. In Britain, a 23% of men and 9% of women indulge in "heavy drinking". Among 16-24 year-olds in Britain, 51% of men and 40% of women drink heavily. In the US, 30% are "binge" or "heavy" drinkers, with the heaviest misuse among 18-29 year-olds. Due to its devastating results and its ability to reach the masses in a manner that illegal drugs cannot, it is the most dangerous drug in our society. Countless lives have been damaged and ruined because of its intoxicating effects. The Prophet ﷺ has said, "Alcohol is the gathering of sin." (Hadith) This is the best description of alcohol. When consumed, alcohol can bring together various sins.

On a daily basis we hear and see many stories in the media about a husband who became drunk and beat his wife: in the UK, 37% of domestic violence cases involve alcohol, while in the US two-thirds reported that alcohol was a factor. In the UK, there were a million alcohol-fuelled violent attacks in 2007/8, 45% of the total, while, in the US, it was a factor in a fifth of cases. The US Department of Justice reports that about a third of convicted criminals are found to have committed their crimes while under the influence of alcohol, while the UK Home Office crime survey (2007/8) found that the top three factors thought to cause crime were lack of parental discipline as well as drug and alcohol misuse. Despite these obvious bad effects of alcohol, people still try to justify their actions. The common justification given is that alcohol in small quantities is harmless and in fact, healthy – people will cite medical reports stating the health benefits of drinking alcohol.

It is important to note as believers that we do not question the veracity of these reports. In fact, Allah ﷻ says:

> **They ask you about alcohol and gambling. Say: "In them are a great sin and a benefit for mankind. But their sin is greater than their benefit."** (2:219)

Allah ﷻ has the Prophet ﷺ tell mankind that there may be a benefit in alcohol, but that the harm resulting from alcohol consumption greatly outweighs any small benefit. This last portion of the aforementioned verse brings to light a very important point about why we do or do not do certain things as Muslims.

How often do we Muslims show an inferiority complex? If we cannot find an answer when challenged to justify our beliefs, we can make excuses such as, "you don't really have to practice this," or "this isn't necessary in our religion," or, even worse, "this was for people who lived 1,400 years ago." These disrespectful, degrading comments do nothing but denigrate Islam, making it appear an outdated and illegitimate religion.

As believers, our role is to be the slaves and servants of Allah ﷻ, as those who submit and surrender to the will and wisdom of our Creator. Thus, in situations in which we are asked about areas in our religion that may be confusing to non-Muslims, our role is to realize that when Allah ﷻ has given an order, we must first of all accept it and follow it regardless of whether or not we can explain it on other grounds. In that same light, alcohol is haram regardless of whatever small benefits may lie in it because Allah ﷻ has forbidden its consumption in the Qur'an. We are bound to believe that Allah ﷻ cares for us, as our Creator knows our natures better than we do, and is the best judge of what ultimately benefits and harms us, such as the case of prohibition of alcohol. Yet, at the same time, the reasoning and evidence for alcohol having a harmful impact on society is clear enough.

There are many celebrities who could not find contentment in their money or fame and subsequently turned to drug abuse such as Lindsey Lohan, Kurt Cobain, Courtney Love, Amy Winehouse, Snoop Dogg, David Hasselhoff, Marilyn Monroe and Elvis Presley have grown to become household names. Drugs and alcohol were meant to fill a void in these celebrity lives that even their wealth and popularity could not fill. Drugs and alcohol became an easy escape, drowning their worries with a high they thought would last but didn't.

As youth in this society, we too can relate to that feeling of wanting to escape from the pressures that are constantly thrown on our shoulders. This is why many people we know may have already turned to drugs for their escape. The problem is that after the high there is always a horrible low.

The escape that people are seeking never lasts and they end up looking for a new high. As a result, they go back and do more drugs to try to get that high again.

As believers, we need to understand that Allah ﷻ grants us a certain elation that is unmatched by any other thing in this world, and that is the ecstasy of faith. So many people chase after drugs and alcohol in order to find happiness and to fill a void that they feel they cannot fill in any other way. But imagine the type of happiness that the companions of the Prophet ﷺ must have felt where despite the fact that many of them lived in a state of complete poverty, many of them were beaten and tortured for their belief, and many of them were boycotted because of their faith – yet they still refused to give up their religion. Their firmness in faith was a result of the pleasure and joy that they found in the din and had never experienced before. As a result, they were able to give away their wealth and struggle through immense difficulties for the sake of Allah ﷻ.

In fact, before the prohibition of alcohol we find that some of the Sahabah used to drink. When the verse was revealed explicitly banning alcohol, the companions began to throw out their wine and drop the glasses of alcohol that were in their hands. Those who were in the act of drinking their wine began to spit it out. Why? Because they knew the pleasure they received from, in this case, alcohol was nothing compared to the joy they attained by pleasing Allah ﷻ. These examples are not just stories but real-life examples of how the din brings such an ecstasy in the lives of people that they would give up their lives and their comfort for the sake of obeying Allah ﷻ faithfully.

What we have to understand is that this is not far-fetched. If we try hard and submit sincerely to Allah ﷻ we too can experience this feeling. Many of us can attest to the fact that there was some point and time in our lives where we may have heard a lecture, prayed a prayer, made a du'a, or sat in the month of Ramadan (the ninth month on the lunar calendar in which Muslims are ordered to fast from dawn to sunset) when tears begin rolling down our cheeks, shivers run up our spine, and we feel an immense feeling of closeness to Allah ﷻ. This is the first taste of the din that Allah ﷻ gives us to experience a glimpse of the ecstasy that we can feel through religion. But, unlike drugs, there isn't a crash after the high. All we have to do to maintain this high is worship Allah ﷻ, and that's for free.

PRACTICAL SOLUTIONS

- Do not put yourself in a situation where your peers are drinking or doing drugs.
- If you have tried alcohol or drugs, repent and ask Allah ﷻ to forgive you and shield you from these vices.
- Do not sell drugs or alcohol.
- Try to work at a place where alcohol is not the main source of income like a bar or brewery, etc.
- Make du'a that Allah ﷻ gives you halal provisions. You should start your du'a with Allah's names al-Muqit (the Sustainer) and al-Razaq (the Provider) and pray that Allah ﷻ provides you sustenance that is halal and beneficial.

8

The Rhythm's Gonna Get You
Music

What! We know what you're thinking: "*everything* is haram". Music is everywhere in our society and very much a part of our lives. Music can make a person who is down feel better, prepare athletes for competition, and generally alter an individual's mood. In movies, music is used to frame scenes. For example, if a scene is full of suspense, then the background music rises and builds up; if it is an action-packed scene then the music has a faster tempo. In clubs, music can quite literally make our bodies move. Before getting into whether music is halal or haram, we want to look at music itself.

One of the rare things about listening to music is that it is not an exclusive activity, compared to other issues we cover in this book. An individual can do other things while listening to music like driving, doing homework, playing sport, and so on. This is one reason why music is so prevalent today.

The main problem with music is how greatly we allow it to encompass us. Is it that every time we get into the car, we turn on the radio? Compare how many music CDs we have with Islamic lectures or Qur'an CDs. Which ones do we listen to more often? Better yet, let's examine the play lists on our MP3 players. Just having lectures or Qur'an on our MP3 player is not sufficient. How many songs can we sing? How many lyrics have we memorized? On the other hand, how much of the Qur'an have we learned? Do the songs we listen to make us want to watch the accompanying music videos? Does the music we listen to have sexually-explicit lyrics or other inappropriate content? Do any of these songs mention things against the teachings of Islam? Do the musicians we listen to help dictate the way we talk or dress, or influence whom we choose to hang out with? What we need do is to think about how much music affects us. Is it bringing us closer to Allah ﷻ or pushing us further away from Him? Does it make us think about things that remind us of Allah ﷻ or about things that are against His commands?

Music itself has effects on us that we should be wary of. Lyrics are often essential to the enjoyment of a song. We often hear people saying that the words to a song are deep or they hit them hard. In fact, many people go so far as to explain why certain lyrics are spiritual or Islamic. But what type of lifestyle and values are these songs promoting? Sometimes the overall content of a song may be sending out the wrong message. People will argue that we are exposed to questionable values and behaviour on a daily basis at school; therefore, it's already a part of their lives. However, an initial exposure doesn't legitimize further exposure. Lyrics that speak about getting with a girl or a guy, doing drugs, having sex, killing, and whatever other topics exist today go against all Islamic principles. The problem is that these lyrics are often not as harmless as we may often think.

Have we ever thought about why commercials on the radio are not just spoken? Or why specific slogans by companies are accompanied by a jingle? The reason is simple: music becomes embedded in the mind. Any time music accompanies something, the resulting combination will get into our heads. That is why we may hear a song and it will remind us of an incident or moment in our lives and it feels as if we are reliving it. This same idea applies to the lyrics we listen to. If we just listen to lyrics without any music we would probably struggle to remember the words. However, with music, the lyrics become ingrained in our minds. Common sense and experience tell us that when something is ingrained in the mind, a person may be influenced by the ideas behind the lyrics.

When the songs we listen to are filled with swearing and promote sin, we can only listen to so much before the message begins to influence what we think is normal and may even influence our behaviour. Now Islam completely prohibits swearing. It comes in a hadith related by Imam Tirmidhi ﷺ , a famous scholar of hadith, that the Prophet ﷺ forbade us from using foul language. We mention this because a lot of popular music has foul language, and our listening to this type of language is completely haram. The content of the songs we listen to make a lasting imprint on our hearts.

Dr. Jawad Shah, a neuro-surgeon residing in Flint, Michagan, and also a famous and reputed speaker about various topics within Islam, once told Sa'ad – after he was discharged from the hospital following his life-threatening accident – that when people are unconscious they begin to say random things that they do not remember speaking about when they become conscious. He notes that when people are unconscious, whatever is in their mind and heart begins manifesting itself on their tongues. Dr. Shah's observations indicate how people ultimately reveal much of what is reverberating in their hearts either quite obviously through their tongues or in their daily actions. This explanation also brings to light an incident regarding one of Sa'ad's teachers in *madrasa*, a traditional Islamic school of learning, who had surgery, and, as a result, was unconscious for a period of time. During this time the doctors heard him saying and singing strange things that they could not understand. When he awoke the doctors asked him what he was saying. He responded by telling them that he obviously does not know what he was saying, but he would not be surprised if he was reciting the Qur'an. The reason for this was because he never left the Qur'an while he was conscious, so he would not expect the Qur'an to leave him in his time of need. *SubhanAllah*! Glory be to Allah! This is the result of having only pure things inside his heart.

Returning back to the topic, we all know according to Islam, people are not supposed to tell others about the sins they commit. What else do these people rap or sing about?

Many lyrics deal with what they did or what they plan on doing. Exposing our sins or even our inclination towards sin goes against our human nature. No one would like to be embarrassed and have their more shameful moments exposed.

And surely we have honoured the children of Adam. (17:70)

If we were honoured by Allah ﷻ, why are we so quick to disgrace ourselves?

Beyond the messages touted in songs, the sounds within the music have profound effects on our hearts as well. The beats and melodies resonate throughout our hearts and minds and will shape us as people. This is what attracts most people to listen to songs. How would it be to watch a music video while the volume was muted? Think about this question. We probably can not imagine watching people dance or strut to a beat without the music. They would look ridiculous! It would also be strange if they were merely dancing to the words of a song without any music or beat. It is clear in this example that in most cases the instrumental portion of the music is essential. Without it, the song would not be as appealing. Now let's examine the Islamic perspective on music.

Islamically, lyrics that are proper and do not include foul language or improper content are permissible. Historically, we see that the Sahabah did sing and chant, but they did not use musical instruments. The only permitted type of musical accompaniment that we find in hadith is the *duff*, a percussion instrument which is a drum covered with a skin on one side only. The duff was only used in rare occasions, such as war. Islamic scholars comment on such use of instruments and have varying opinions regarding it. A small minority of scholars feel that all musical instruments are permissible, whereas some scholars feel that all percussion instruments are permissible. Finally, the remaining scholars feel that only a duff can be used and even that is only for specified occasions, and even, in those situations, using only a certain beat. While we are not proclaiming any one view as being correct, we can look at the Hadith for guidance. The Prophet ﷺ mentioned, "Bells (music) are the instruments of Satan." (Hadith) In another Hadith the Prophet ﷺ warned us, "Music causes hypocrisy to grow in the hearts as water causes plants to grow." (Hadith)

The first Hadith displays the enticing manner in which Shaytan uses musical instruments against us, while the latter Hadith, which is even scarier, shows that music causes hypocrisy to grow in our hearts. The hypocrites, according to the Qu'ran, are in the worst situation in the hereafter.

Indeed the hypocrites are in the lowest level of the hellfire. (4:145)

Although listening to music does not make us complete hypocrites, why would we want to share any semblance with the hypocrites existing within our lives? We want to distance ourselves from every person heading toward the hellfire, especially those approaching its lowest level.

In an explanation given by Shaykh Husain Abdul Sattar on this particular Hadith, he mentions the example of our hearts being like a garden that can be cultivated. Anyone who gardens knows that one of the biggest enemies a garden faces is weeds. By allowing music to seep into our hearts, we unknowingly begin to allow weeds to flourish in our garden. As a result, the potential beauty that our heart can reach is ruined by the presence of these weeds. Anyone who has tried to remove weeds knows that when we pull them up, they are not easy to take out. They have put down roots in the garden. What this shows is that much of the damage is done to a garden before the weeds even appear on the surface. In that same way, much of the damage is done by music before the traces of hypocrisy become apparent in our actions. Thus, if this is the effect music has on our hearts and on our akhirah, despite the deep attachment we have with it, we will find greater benefit in leaving it.

- Cut down on listening to music.
- Listen to songs (nashids) by Islamic groups.
- Stop listening to music that uses profanity, degrades women, and promotes un-Islamic behaviour.
- Ask yourself:
  - Do you turn on the radio every time you get into the car?
  - How many music CDs do you own and how many Islamic lectures or Qur'an CDs do you have?
  - If you have the same amount, then which one do you listen to more often?
  - How many songs have you memorized?
  - How much Qur'an have you learned?
  - Do the songs you listen to make you want to watch music videos?
  - Does the music you listen to have explicit lyrics or inappropriate content?
  - Do any songs that you listen to mention things that are against the rules of Islam?
  - Do the musicians you listen to affect the way you talk or dress or influence your decisions about whom you hang with?
  - Is the music getting you closer to Allah ﷻ or further away from Him?
- Make du'a that Allah ﷻ gives us good judgement so that we don't listen to what is harmful to us. Begin your du'a by remembering Allah's names: al-Hadi (The Guide) and al-Sami' (The Hearer).

Parents Just Don't Understand
Parents

"Man, *my* parents are stubborn and old school – they don't understand society." Sound familiar? Yes, it is true that many of our parents are immigrants who, while growing up, did not face these temptations: clubs, TV, internet, dating, and so on. In many of their countries, these vices only exist discreetly. As for this society, these troubles might actually come to us rather than us having to seek them out. Parents are scared about what will happen to us and, as parents ourselves, we can attest to the fact that their fears come only from a deep love and concern. Sure, it may feel annoying to hear our parents' complaints on what is haram or not, but remember, it is their duty to raise us correctly, and we become a test for them as well.

Know that your wealth and your children are a test. (8:28)

Every kid at one time or another feels annoyed, angry and even impatient with their parents. But being angry gets us nowhere. Communication, on the other hand, can be the key. Why not try explaining to them what is going on? We know you must be thinking, "What do you want me to tell them? That I like girls or I was asked to go to a party? Are you crazy?" We know this may be asking too much, but at least let them know that you understand they are worried and know what they want is the best for you. Once we connect with our parents in this manner, they will be more inclined to understand our reasons to want to do various things. The more we fall out with our parents, argue with them, or try to hide things from them, the less they will trust us, which will lead them to be more reluctant to allow us the freedom to make choices.

For example, what is the one thing parents insist upon most when their kid goes out? Call! If we're running late, all they want is a phone call. If we have arrived safely to our destination, they just want a simple phone call telling them so. When he was younger, Habeeb had the opportunity to travel to California and Arizona with an all-star traveling team for basketball. One of the conditions his parents made before they would approve the trip was that he would have to call in the morning and at night from his hotel room. This agreement helped relieve his parents' concerns for his well-being and, at the same time, gave him the opportunity to play in the tournament and have a great time. Here we have a win-win situation.

Also, talking with our parents allows them to ask questions as well: "Who are the people you are hanging out with? What are their names? Who are their parents? Do they go to the *masjid*?" These questions may be annoying but are legitimate questions that parents have the right to ask. They need to know how and with whom we are spending the majority of our free time. Remember, "You will be (in the hereafter) with those whom you love." (Hadith)

Allah ﷻ says in the Qur'an:

> **Your Lord has decreed to you that you worship none other than Him, and that you show kindness to your parents.** (17:23)

The reason why this is important is that such an order is not restricted to only *Surah al-Isra'*, the seventeenth chapter of the Qur'an. If we look at *Surah al-Baqarah*, the second chapter of the Qur'an, alongside other chapters, Allah ﷻ is constantly reminding the believers to worship Him and then to act with kindness towards their parents.

There is a concept in Islam known as *tartib* (order). Tartib exists in all acts of worship. For example, people are not permitted to perform a *sajdah* (prostration) prior to *qiyam* (standing) in prayer. Also, people are not supposed to wash their feet prior to their hands in *wudu'* (ablution). In that regard, whenever Allah ﷻ gives a command in the Qur'an, paying close attention to it is crucial for us. When Allah ﷻ tells man to obey Him and then follows this with another command, directing us to show kindness to our parents, it shows that Allah ﷻ requires our obedience and loyalty to be first and foremost towards Him and secondly towards our parents. This is the elevated status that Allah ﷻ has given parents in Islam.

There is a story of a Sahabi who came to the Prophet ﷺ and told him that he had performed the entire act of *Hajj*, the pilgrimage to Makkah that every believer is required to do once in a lifetime, with his mother on his back because she was too old and weak to walk. He then asked the Prophet ﷺ if he had fulfilled the right of his mother. The Prophet ﷺ responded by telling him he had not even compensated for one contraction that his mother suffered while giving birth to him.

> *We have commanded man to treat his parents kindly. His mother bore him with hardship and gave birth to him with hardship.* (46:15)

SubhanAllah, imagine the Hajj 1400 years ago. There were no buses taking people back and forth from Makkah to Mina, then to Arafat and Muzdalifah, the various places that need to be visited when performing Hajj. Nor were there air-conditioned tents or *masajid* (mosques). The two hillocks of Safa and Marwa that Hajra ﷺ ran up and down when searching for water to quench her thirst and enable her to feed her son, Isma'il ﷺ, were not shaded from the sun as they are today. In those testing conditions, the Sahabi carried his mother through the entire Hajj. And, even after all of this, he still did not return the sacrifice she had made by giving birth to him and raising him.

We chose to include this story because, while parents can and will be difficult, we still must always remember the position Allah ﷻ has given them in our lives. Sometimes asking them to understand us and for us to understand them will not be easy. If we can recall Allah's command upon us we will realize our parents possess a key to *Jannah* (heaven) for us. After all, "Paradise is under the feet of your mother." (Hadith) So let us try to grow closer to them and be of greater service to them in order to attain Allah's pleasure.

We should sympathize with our parents: they may not understand our struggle as second or third-generation Muslims in America or Britain, but also we do not understand their difficulties in raising children in a foreign land. Our parents are faced with the fear of losing their heritage and culture in this nation and the effects that will have on our din. What can we do to give our parents comfort regarding this matter? Remember that "The pleasure of your father is the pleasure of your Lord, and the anger of your father is the anger of your Lord." (Hadith)

We can simply talk to them. For example, when we were in elementary school, we used to tell our parents *everything* from what we did during our free time to what our teachers said in class to what happened at lunch, what we had for homework, and so on until our parents wished we would stop talking. Then, all of a sudden, when we reach junior high or secondary school, our conversation went more like the following:

Parents: "How was your day?"
Us: "Good."
Parents: "How was school?"
Us: "Boring."
Parents: "What did you do today at school?"
Us: "Nothing."
Parents: "What would you like for dinner?"
Us: "Anything."

This sudden, drastic change from being extra-talkative to not saying anything beyond one or two words naturally raises the concern and curiosity of our parents. We may think, "What's the difference?" or "It's none of their business anyway." But we need to be realistic and recognize how suspicious this uncommunicative behaviour may look to our parents, especially since most of them did not come from a culture where young adults could go into their own room and close the door on the rest of the family.

A person's culture and lineage is their identity, and when it does not conflict with Islam, it should be honoured. Needless to say our Muslim identity is preferred over all others. As for our parents, they left their homes and countries in order to give us a better life. Out of a concern to hold on to the security they had back in their homelands, parents begin to enforce the rules and ways they had experienced and were taught. It's understandable: after all, as they have never experienced another kind of upbringing. Thus, we need to be understanding of them, and, inshaAllah, Allah ﷻ will also make them understanding towards us. For such people there is great reward.

Such are the people from whom We shall accept the best of their deeds and overlook their wrongdoings. (46:16)

PRACTICAL SOLUTIONS

- Have good communication with your parents.
- Thank your parents for the things they provide for you.
- If you have a disagreement, try to understand their side. If you cannot make them understand, try to get a relative or a friend who can talk to your parents.
- Make du'a for your parents.
- Let your parents meet your friends for this will ease their worries.
- Call and tell your parents where you are, especially call when you are running late.
- Show affection to your father or mother. Give them a hug or a kiss at least once a week.
- Remind them that you love them.
- Help around the house. Take out the garbage, mow the lawn, set the table for dinner, wash the dishes, etc.
- Follow the rules of your house.
- Respect your parents' cultural traditions. There are many good qualities to learn from tradition. So long as they do not contradict the laws of Islam, follow your parents' wishes.
- If you disagree with your parents, make sure not to respond when you are angry.
- Give your parents gifts on Eid or at any other time. Even if it is small, it will go a long way.

My Clique, My Crew, My Peeps
Keeping Company

It is human nature to socialize with and to have friends; we all have friends. In studying the life of the Prophet 鷺, it is noteworthy that after he began receiving revelation he would never travel alone: he was always with somebody. The people who were by his side were guaranteed the highest place in heaven. These fortunate individuals, the Sahabah, were blessed to have spent time in the company of the greatest human being.

The Prophet 鷺 always had companions with him wherever he went. In fact, if you look at the two greatest journeys the Prophet 鷺 had taken, namely the *hijrah* (migration, in this context it refers to the migration from Makkah to Madinah) and the *isra* and *mi'raj* (the night journey and ascension, in this context it refers to the night journey that the Prophet 鷺 made from Makkah to Jerusalem, then to the heavens), both companions he had for these two life-changing journeys were the best possible companions: Abu Bakr 羨, the greatest of all the companions, and the Angel Jibril 鷺, the greatest of all the angels. For us, the greatest journey we will make is the journey of life, and our destination, *insha'Allah*, will be heaven. Thus, in our everyday travels, everything is on the line and it is crucial that we have the best possible companions.

We tend to lean towards individuals who we can talk to, ask advice of, hang out with, and generally have things in common with. But the question is: are our friends individuals who help us get closer to Allah ﷻ or pull us away from Him? When the prayer is due, do our friends make us delay or miss our prayer or remind us of it? Is this an individual who helps us to plan a date or a party or who tries to talk us out of it? Do our friends show us websites or music we would not listen to if they had not shown us? If our parents knew some of the things we were doing with this person would they be upset? Just because many of our friends are Muslim does not mean that we will not be tempted. All of us are responsible for our own actions. But sometimes putting ourselves in a situation will increase our chances of doing something wrong. If all of our friends want to go to a party, what are we going to say? What are we going to do?

Sometimes peer pressure and the image our friends have of us seems more crucial than the way our parents see us. Everyone wants to belong to something or someone. For example, gang members feel a sense of purpose and security as part of their crew. It's usually too late for most gang members once they actually start to regret being part of a gang – many lose their lives or end up in jail before realizing the error of their ways. Kids who start smoking do so because their friends are doing it. They try once, then twice, and then eventually get addicted to it. Not too many kids just buy cigarettes by themselves and try smoking alone. A majority of the time, it is friends who influence this decision. We need to be honest with ourselves and be aware that Shaytan will make us think that we need to keep hanging out with these friends in order to change them or help them. But be really careful: even if you have a strong, resilient personality that does not mean your *iman* (faith) is strong enough to avoid temptation while trying to help out your friends.

The Day of Judgment will be a very scary scene. All that we know as security in this world will leave us, and we will be left with our deeds which will be accounted for. Among the various securities that will be taken away from us is the security of those closest to us. In this world we see our parents as pillars of strength and support. But the difficulties of the Day of Judgment will even make some parents abandon their children, and some children abandon their parents.

On the Day when a person runs from his brother, and his mother and his father and his companion and his kids. For every person on that Day shall have enough concern to make him indifferent to others. (80:34-37)

In fact, the closer the relationships in this world, the more worried we will be in the hereafter as we will remember all of the times we have wronged these people. The Prophet ﷺ said that about the Day of Judgment, "A person will be with whom he loves." (Hadith) Those whom we loved in this world will surround us in the hereafter. The question lies in whether or not that person's influence on us was beneficial or detrimental. If he or she was good company, then we will join them in heaven. If he or she was bad company, then may Allah ﷻ have mercy on us all.

When we constantly seek company with a group of people, we naturally seek to be more like them and act like them. Even in our lives we can think of countless examples of people who we thought would never smoke or be involved with drugs. Most likely when asked, these people attribute their habits and addictions to the company they've kept. Though they never intended to begin smoking or doing drugs, they succumbed to the influence of their friends partaking in these acts. The Prophet ﷺ highlighted this principle beautifully when he relayed a situation regarding surrounding oneself with certain types of friends. The first example deals with a person whose friend sells *'itr* (non-alcoholic perfume). Either his friend will give him 'itr to try on, or he will merely benefit from the scent in the store. Through both scenarios he will leave his friend having been perfumed by the scent in the store. The second example deals with a person whose friend is a blacksmith. Either he will work with his friend, perspiring and becoming sooty from the kiln, or, if he does not work with his friend, the suffocating environment will cause him to leave in a similar state.

A similar anecdote to this exists today. If we hang out with a friend who smokes, even if we do not smoke ourselves, the smell will get in our clothes and we will get hurt through second-hand smoking. In the end, it is clear that we will either benefit or be harmed by the company we keep.

PRACTICAL SOLUTIONS

Your answers to the following questions may, insha' Allah, help you to make the best decisions on who to hang with:

- Are your friends helping you to be a better Muslim?
- Are your friends individuals who strive to become better themselves?
- Are your friends constantly getting in trouble?
- Are your friends people that Allah ﷺ is likely to be happy with?
- Are your friends people who are following a pathway to Jannah or *Jahannam* (hell) in the hereafter?

Dress to Impress
Clothing

"Clothing makes the man" – this popular cliché contains little substance but much truth. Various aspects of our lives reveal parts of our personality to the world – the books we read, the company we keep, the courses we study – but, one of the most telling statements we make is through the clothing we wear. Many of us feel we dress in a way that is religiously appropriate but just as many of us can't answer for certain: "What is Islamic clothing?" For women, is it wearing *hijab* (headscarf), *jilbab* (full-length loose garment), *niqab* (face veil)? Is it wearing *shalwar qameez*, the Indo-Pakistani long shirt and loose pants? For men, is it wearing a *thawb* (a full-length loose garment), a *kufi* (skullcap), or an *imamah* (turban)? Many people feel these things are part of the Sunnah, while others feel they are cultural and do not have anything to do with Islam. While this has been subject to discussion and debate for years, and neither of us are scholars who can give a definitive answer, there are certain principles of the Sunnah we can establish as guidelines to follow in our lives.

Before we discuss our opinions on clothing, we need to see what the Qur'an says about this topic. Allah ﷻ says in Surah al-A'raf:

> *Oh children of Adam, surely we have sent down upon you clothing to cover your shame and for beauty; and the clothing of taqwa (consciousness of Allah), that is the best. That is from the signs of Allah so that you may remember.*
> (Qur'an 7:26)

Allah ﷻ clarifies in this verse that clothes have been given to us by Allah ﷻ for the purpose of covering our shame, which, according to the scholars means to cover those parts of the body which are not to be exposed publicly, and to beautify us. Thus, the clothes we wear have the primary responsibility of covering our bodies and not revealing to others how our bodies look.

When it comes to dress there are general principles that are applicable to both males and females. Both genders are required to wear loose and modest clothing. Although this may not seem like a big deal, an epidemic of shrinking clothes is spreading rapidly today. Perhaps there is a gigantic washer-dryer processing that all clothes pass through before they hit the stores and this machine has shrunk all clothing. Most clothing at retail is fitted to expose the body's shape. Women purchase jeans that leave nothing to the imagination and men wear what is popularly referred to as "muscle shirts" to expose their physiques. Islamically speaking, such clothing is not permissible.

Islam not only requires us to cover ourselves, but to cover ourselves with clothes that are loose. Why is it insufficient to cover ourselves in any manner? Well, it's quite simple. The body's shape that would otherwise have been hidden is defined by tight clothing, and if the clothes are tight enough the person is seen as virtually naked as the body's shape is highly visible even if technically it's covered. The Prophet ﷺ said there would be people who wear clothing but appear naked – a statement that is very much true today. It is incumbent upon us to stay away from this practice of dressing as it displeased the Prophet ﷺ, which means it displeases Allah ﷻ. The clothing one wears should not only be loose but long so that it also drapes over the body – especially between the navel and the knees.

Furthermore, we should never wear clothing that imitates the opposite gender as the Prophet ﷺ clearly banned it. Although many of the clothes worn by men and women today are similar or "gender-neutral", a guiding principle to always keep in mind is that clothing obviously for one gender should be left to that gender. In this regard, materials such as silk and gold are prohibited for men. Also, the clothing we wear should not be aimed at attracting the opposite gender: our clothing should reflect a modest disposition.

Now that the general principles have been addressed, we can look at the separate rulings for men and women. Guys, yes, we have a little more leeway, but we should understand that some parents and community members have problems with the way we dress. Many of us wear jerseys and shorts to Friday prayer. This is a day when Allah ﷻ commands us to leave everything and come for prayer; this is a day where we should wear our best clothing. We can argue we are wearing our most expensive clothes, but do we really feel this is the best clothing to wear in front of Allah ﷻ on a day that has been given extra importance. If we try to follow all the traditions of the Prophet ﷺ, why would you want to wear sportswear? Would we wear such clothes to a job interview or a graduation?

The One who invites us on Fridays is better than any person: He is the Creator of the worlds. We should try everything possible to impress Him. If we must wear shorts, then these should at least be knee-length. We need to realize even when praying in long shorts, if you go in to the sitting position some shorts may ride up past the knees. Also, this is insensitive to sisters who, in hot weather, are wearing long sleeve shirts, pants, long skirts, *jilbab*s, and *hijab*s.

Muslims living as a minority in a non-Muslim country face certain obstacles and difficulties that cause us to feel that Islam is difficult. While practicing Islam may not be easy for everyone, we should remember that even more difficult times came to those who preceded us. In fact, Allah ﷻ mentions this in the Qur'an, explaining that getting into heaven is not necessarily easy.

Do you think that entering Heaven is easy? When there came examples of people who came before you. We tried them with trials and calamities and disasters until the

Prophet and those who were with him said "Where is the help of Allah?" Verily the Help of Allah is near. (2:214)

So dressing properly sometimes puts us in uncomfortable situations in which people look at us differently. No one wants to feel strange and left out, but there are great rewards for the person who stands firm on the teachings of Islam despite being socially slighted or even mocked.

The second factor that should give us strength when in such situations is our brothers and sisters in Islam. A Muslim brother or sister should be a source of comfort and support to help us through the most difficult times. Imagine how a sister feels when she is willingly covering herself for the sake of pleasing Allah ﷻ and she sees her Muslim brother enjoying the weather by covering only the bare minimum. Yes, it is true a brother is obligated to cover less, but that doesn't mean he should take every opportunity to wear the least clothing possible. In fact, brothers should work on their modesty as well by covering themselves. Not only will this help to increase a brother's piety, but this act will also show care for our Muslim sisters and the challenges they endure. The latter may seem unimportant, but we all know how empowering it is to know our friends and siblings support us. In that same light, our sisters in Islam want to feel their brothers support them and that means taking the extra effort to dress more modestly and to share in their struggle.

Unfortunately we have noticed more and more brothers partaking in a fashion trend that completely defies all efforts toward modesty. This ridiculous phenomenon is pant-sagging, and you all know what we're talking about here. There are two explanations for how this trend started and both, ironically, began in the prison system. The first explanation is that pant-sagging stems from the practice of men in prison claiming other inmates as their "property". After claiming someone, the "pimps" in the prison would have the person stain their boxers with a specific juice color pertaining to their owner and force them to wear their pants sagged so others would know that they had been claimed. Imagine how upon being released from prison these men must feel when they see a boy on the street with sagged pants. The second explanation is that pant-sagging is a result of how inmates are not allowed to wear belts with their pants because of the threat of suicide. What we should wonder about is why are we trying to imitate the dregs of society?

Furthermore, Allah ﷻ and the Prophet ﷺ would never sanction showing our boxers to everyone. They have encouraged us to be modest in our actions and dress, as it is part of our way of life. As a Hadith says, "Modesty is a branch of faith." Islam is a religion of modesty; exposing our undergarments is not a modest way of dressing. We should be so concerned about our din and how well we are adhering to Islamic values as we will be judged for our decisions in this regard.

Additionally, worrying about the state of our own din should leave us with little time to focus on and criticize others for the way they dress. People who wear a *thawb*, *shalwar qameez* or a *kufi* should not be ridiculed. If they are wearing this clothing to come closer to Allah ﷻ and follow the Sunnah of the Prophet ﷺ, then more power to them. Some might say that we should dress as everyone else dresses, especially since this country has given so much to us. But should we place our desire to fit into society above our duty towards our din? Who was it that paid a hefty price to make sure that we are able to practice Islam today? When we look at it in that light, it is much more difficult to look down on our brothers who try to dress according to the Sunnah. As long as brothers who wear kufis don't force it upon others or look down on others who do not, then we should be supportive. We have seen too many people on both sides: those who dress according to the Sunnah and feel people who do not are lost or have less iman, and those who wear westernized clothing who look at people with traditional clothing as fanatics and extremists. No matter where our preference lies, we should always remember that people "dress to impress". The same is true with Muslims, except that we "dress to impress Allah".

As for women, the rulings relating to clothing and modesty are much more detailed. Without going into specific differences of opinion, the minimum that women should adhere to is as follows: women are permitted to reveal their hands, face, and feet, and should cover the body with loose, modest clothing that does not reveal the shape of the body. Often times we see sisters who wear hijab but their clothing is very tight and revealing. While we commend sisters for taking the step of wearing the hijab, we stress the importance of not wearing tight clothing. Modesty comes from the heart: when we dress ourselves in the morning, we should ask ourselves if we look like a Muslim and have made a sincere effort to dress in a manner that is pleasing to Allah ﷻ. Then maybe at that point we will realize it's probably better to throw a jacket over the shirt we are wearing or replace it with a looser garment.

There is no doubt that wearing the hijab in a non-Muslim society is difficult. In fact, some people have gone so far as to say that it is not incumbent upon us in a non-Muslim society. Although this statement should not be taken by anyone, it does shed some light – especially for brothers – on how difficult the hijab really is. At the same time, sisters can take comfort in the great reward Allah ﷻ will likely bestow upon them in the hereafter for following the din. Instead of abandoning the hijab and losing this tradition, Muslim women have decided to wear it and have, in essence, become pioneers of this practice in America, Britain and elsewhere.

Ten years ago many non-Muslims did not even know the headscarf was called a hijab, but today people are quickly becoming familiar with it. While perhaps we have a long way to go before hjiab becomes accepted as mainstream, it is important for Muslim women to stand tall and be proud of their decision to wear the headscarf. Your confidence will help you to gain the respect you deserve and provide better opportunities to educate people about your decision to wear hijab. Most importantly, know that each time you wear the headscarf you are gaining Allah's pleasure and His pleasure should be what a Muslim should aspire to gain.

Beyond the hijab, there is the issue for women about clothing in general. To jilbab or not to jilbab – that is the question. To some women it's simply easier to throw on this garment over their regular American-style clothes and run out the door. But for others, especially girls born and raised in the West who identify more with this culture have found creative ways to dress Islamically in mainstream American fashions – they don long, loose shirts over wide-leg pants or floor-length skirts and achieve the same effect as a jilbab. What is crucial to remember if you are not already practicing a properly modest, Islamic form of dressing, is you should make the proper intention to dress to gain Allah's pleasure, and pray to Him to gain the strength to do so and work toward that goal, progressing on your path.

Last but not least, modest dressing does not mean sloppy dressing. The Prophet ﷺ was a tidy and well-dressed man. When you dress thoughtfully, not only do you please Allah ﷺ but you also inspire those around you to follow your Islamic style. People aiming to be more righteous Muslims may begin to take less care of their appearance out of an abandonment of worldly concern – they stop grooming themselves and ironing their clothes. However, people are turned off by such an appearance and begin to associate religiosity with untidiness. As a result, these well-intentioned Muslims who wanted to attain righteousness by not caring for their appearance unknowingly end up turning others away from the din. We understand that they are trying to practice an Islamic virtue known as *zuhd* (abstention, or abstaining from things of this world). Yet, zuhd does not necessarily mean giving up everything in this world. Mufti Minhajuddin Ahmad once defined the term zuhd, and we believe this is something all of us should remember, as not meaning you should have nothing of this world, but that true zuhd means the dunya owns nothing of your heart. In fact, the Prophet ﷺ said, "No one who has an atom's weight of pride in his heart will enter Paradise." A man said, "And if a man likes his clothes to be good and his sandals to be good?" The Prophet ﷺ

replied, "Allah ﷻ is beautiful and loves beauty. Pride means renouncing the truth and belittling people." (Hadith)

As Muslims, we have to take advantage of every opening to bring people closer to Allah ﷻ.

PRACTICAL SOLUTIONS

- Look at your wardrobe and ask yourself, "Is all this appropriate to wear?"
- Ask yourself, "Is my clothing abiding by the commandments of Allah ﷻ?"
- Ask yourself, "Why am I dressing like this. Is it to attract a girl/boy?"
- Don't judge people by the way they dress.
- Look in the mirror and think if you would want your parents to see you leaving the house like that.
- Make the intention to dress appropriately and take steps toward perfecting your goal.

Bling Bling
Showing Off

This is a society that thrives on showing off: showing off how much money a person makes, what clothes a person wears, even showing off who one dates! Take sports stars, actors, actresses and musicians, most live a life of luxury and live that life very publicly. They talk about and display the beautiful things they own. That in itself is a problem. Many of these people will develop a complex in which they feel they have earned these luxuries on their own, and have achieved their fortune by their own hands. As a result, these individuals no longer see that Allah 🕮 has blessed them and so they are ungrateful to Allah 🕮.

As if bragging about and flaunting one's wealth aren't bad enough, what comes after this is jealousy and envy. Enough becomes not enough and you begin to envy those with more than yourself. You may create jealousy in others. Even worse, you begin to belittle those whom you perceive as beneath you. For example, if you purchase a new pair of Nike's, you may tell others to "check this out; it cost so much. I'm the first person to get them. They're limited edition." If Allah 🕮 has blessed you with money, then it is understandable that you purchased such an expensive item. But, we see this quite a bit among younger teenagers – they begin to point out shoes and say things like, "Look at those shoes, they're from Payless," or "Those Nike (or Converse, etc.) are out of style; no player wears them," and they begin to mock the student wearing those shoes. When you make people feel bad for what they are wearing or you make them feel embarrassed, then this is a clear indication you are in need of an ego check. Think about the many examples throughout history of people who would show off and boast and how Allah ﷻ humbled them.

The Qur'an speaks about the Pharaoh, who used to say about himself,

> *I am your lord most high.* (Qur'an 79:24)

Speaking about bling, the Pharaoh had the entire world at his feet. The entire known world feared him; the people of his land submitted to his will and would do anything for him. The riches of the country were brought to him and the most amazing and beautiful palaces were constructed for him. The Egyptian pyramids built with such awe-inspiring accuracy are a testament to the high level of command the Pharaoh held. Now imagine the audacity of a man who enjoyed such bounties from Allah ﷻ, and despite this he proclaimed himself to be Allah! His ingratitude to Allah ﷻ eventually led him to attempt to destroy the din of Allah ﷻ and the prophet of that time, Musa ﷺ. The Pharaoh was blinded by the arrogance he had attained and practically thought himself invincible enough to ride his army through the parted Red Sea. It was during this act of contempt that Allah ﷻ showed the Pharaoh the error of his ways by causing the Red Sea to collapse and drown him with his army. If this was not enough, Allah ﷻ said to him,

> *Ah now! And surely you used to sin before and were from the wrongdoers? This day We shall save your body so that you may be a sign to those who come after.* (Qur'an 10:91-92)

Another example that highlights the dangers of arrogance is the story of Qarun in the Qur'an. Qarun was from the people of Musa ﷺ. Allah ﷻ blessed Qarun with an enormous amount of wealth. Such was his wealth that it is mentioned in the Qur'an,

> *Verily Qarun was from the people of Musa, but he rebelled against them. And We had bestowed upon him such*

treasures that their very keys were heavy for a group of strong men. (28:76)

Imagine how great the wealth of an individual must be that the keys to his wealth were so big and heavy that it took a group of strong men to carry them. The people of his community used to see his wealth and wish they possessed what he possessed. Wise individuals warned him to be grateful to Allah ﷻ and not hoard his wealth; rather, they suggested he use it to grow closer to Allah ﷻ and seek the reward of the hereafter. Qarun did not heed their warnings and was arrogant. As a result of his arrogance,

Then We caused the earth to swallow up him and his house. (Qur'an 28:81)

What is most surprising is that those who envied the wealth that he bragged about said, after seeing his end, that:

Verily it is Allah Who enlarges the provision or restricts it for any of His servants He pleases! Had it not been that Allah was gracious to us, He could have caused the earth to swallow us up! Ah! Those who reject Allah will assuredly never prosper. (Qur'an 28:82)

The people of Musa ﷺ saw the result of a person who was given gifts from Allah and, rather than being grateful, claimed such bounties for himself and boasted to others of having earned it himself. As a result, Allah ﷻ took him from this Earth by having it swallow him whole. Allah ﷻ reminds us beautifully of the self-deception that arrogance involves:

And do not walk arrogantly upon the Earth. Surely you cannot tear the Earth [apart] and you will never be taller than the mountains. (Qur'an 17:37)

Showing off isn't restricted only to displaying our wealth. People often show off skills they have been blessed with. A new phenomenon in sport is showing off and boasting. Previously in basketball or football, when someone made a great play the crowd would go wild, pump their fists, give high fives, and scream out loudly. Now, ordinary basketball has been slowly transformed into street ball or And-1 basketball. The name of the game is no longer only to score points but is to do tricks that not only embarrass the player, but truly humiliate him. The object of sport is now to "break someone's ankles," and then point out that you did it. Talking nonsense and making the other individual look foolish is accepted and promoted. In football, scoring a touchdown almost necessitates doing a dance to incite anger from the opposing team. Players have become more concerned with statistics than winning games. What professionals are doing has slowly trickled down to the youth. We, as Muslims, need to be careful we keep humble when doing anything, including playing sport because too much talking nonsense and showing off may result in Allah ﷻ Himself humbling us.

Another example, which is more subtle, is our human tendency to want to gain acceptance and respect from others by revealing our intelligence or skills in a less obvious way. For example, people may find faults in the speakers or scholars, merely to sound smart to others around them. It is one thing to criticize a speech through opinions, saying things like the speaker could have been more passionate and engaging or provided more knowledge or evidence. However, if we feel we could have given a better speech instead and think of running the speaker down, then a problem arises. Although the act of seeking knowledge may have started with a good motive, Shaytan will sneak in and encourage us to tell others that we could have done a better job. The problem is not one of sharing knowledge with others, for to continue discussion of the lecture topic can be extremely beneficial. It is rather when a person wants to be on the centre stage, in the spotlight, in front of thousands of people that the problem of riya' (or showing off) arises.

This tendency also arises when a person acquires some knowledge about Islam or any other topic and begins conversations in order to appear intelligent to others – this obviously constitutes showing off. Another example is if a lecturer makes a small mistake and a person rushes to correct the lecturer primarily for the sake of attracting attention. You should always ask yourself, "Would I be equally satisfied if someone else corrects the speaker or does it have to be me who corrects him?" It's a good sign if someone else can correct the speaker and you don't have a problem with that. But if you feel compelled to correct the speaker, particularly in front of others, then you should be concerned to check your intentions for Shaytan is sneaky. This is not to say that if you see something wrong that you do not offer a correction, but be careful you are not picking on things that are not matters of Islamic law and ethical teaching, as in that case your criticism may merely be a means of appearing better than the person you're criticizing.

There was an incident that involved the two grandsons of the Prophet ﷺ, Hasan and Husayn ؆, and an elderly man. One time, Hasan and Husayn ؆ saw an old man who was not making his wudu' properly. The two brothers decided they would approach the old man to correct him. However, when they approached him, they said they were discussing who made the better wudu' and that they wanted him to judge between them. They both performed wudu' in front of him and then the old man turned to them, smiled, and said that they both did wudu' better than him. The two boys neither mocked the old man nor tried to prove they were better at performing wudu' even though they were younger than him. Rather, they created a situation that allowed the man to be taught without embarrassing him. The old man recognized this and was very grateful.

Another problem with showing off is our desire to be famous or popular. It's not wrong to be sociable or to have friends, of course, but when we like being well-known we have to be careful that we don't become preoccupied with the desire to be closer to people instead of getting closer to Allah ﷻ. We pretend to possess qualities that make people respect and think highly of us, and we try to conceal the flaws in our character instead of trying to cure them. Remember the price of fame. As the saying goes, "don't sell your soul to the devil," for the sake of popularity and fame.

PRACTICAL SOLUTIONS

- If you're blessed with a good appearance, wealth or other things, then be thankful for all that you have and be humble.
- Always question yourself to see why you are doing something and who you are trying to please.
- When you do anything, ask yourself whether it's for the sake of seeking people's approval and praise.
- If you are an Islamic activist, see how your heart reacts if you decline an opportunity and someone else takes up that task like being in charge of a program, speaking, and so on.
- Understand that things do go on without you.
- Always be encouraging towards others who have fewer blessings or less experience than you.
- Remember that being grateful to Allah ﷻ involves using your money, looks, intellect or physical ability for the sake of the good and not for your own ego or desires.

Yo Mama Is So...
Insulting People

As educators, we have seen an increase in negative social interaction. Bullying ranks first among all these hostile interactions. Bullying is a big issue for young people to deal with today, especially in school. For some reason it has become cool to put down and make fun of others. Sometimes people justify this type of bullying by saying they were only joking. The problem is that when we keep making jokes about someone, regardless of who they are, it eventually gets to them, especially if that person is being humiliated in front of other people. This in itself creates another problem – bullied people begin to do things they wouldn't normally do just to avoid being the target of a joke. What is equally worse, they may end up bullying others. Thus, we find many students who change their personalities and the way they dress in order to fit in; many get involved in crime and other bad things they would have stayed away from just to fit in and not be made fun of. What we fail to realize is that by our joking about others in an insulting way – whether it be about their clothes, physical appearance, status, intelligence or ethnicity – we are actually making fun of Allah's creation and what they have been blessed with.

The natural reaction you may be having right now is, "I've asked them, and they said they don't mind." Of course, a joke may be accepted once or twice. But human nature rarely allows us to stop right there because once you end up making a person laugh, it's most likely you will want to then share that same joke with others again to get more laughs.

So not only is that person made fun of but we broadcast that insult to anyone within earshot just for the sake of a laugh, all at the expense of another person's feelings and reputation. We had a few friends who we always called by particular nicknames. Over time, many people started calling them by these names. It was only after several years that they shared their disdain for these nicknames with us – they didn't want anyone, including us, calling them by these names. Imagine that – for almost two decades these brothers kept quiet because they didn't want to be seen as moaners. The joker may get a chance to have everyone's attention, but, for the person being made fun of, rancour and hatred can settle into his heart. After all, no one likes to get laughed at.

According to Imam Tirmidhi, the Prophet ﷺ said, "Whoever makes fun of his brother because of a sin of which he has already repented, will surely commit the same sin during his life." (Hadith)

Furthermore, Allah ﷻ says in the Qur'an,

Oh you who believe, let not one group ridicule another group, for perhaps the latter may be better than the former. Nor should any women ridicule other women who may be better than themselves. And do not find fault with one another or insult each other with derogatory nicknames. (Qur'an 49:11)

These seemingly insignificant comments and jokes, especially calling people by unwanted nicknames often leads to un-expected and undesired results. Those ridiculed hate those who ridicule them. Friendships can be and have been destroyed by such behaviour. Furthermore, these slights tend to be aimed at individuals who are the least deserving or least able and willing to defend themselves.

For example, how many times have we made comments about people with a physical or intellectual disability? Let's be honest, we've all done it at some point. We should be ashamed of ourselves if we cross this line. Allah ﷻ has made all of us with specific bodies and mental capacities. The majority of us have been created with fully functioning bodies and intellectual capacities, and such a great gift from Allah ﷻ should necessitate that we feel extremely grateful for this blessing. Unfortunately, since this gift is so common, we often overlook this blessing until something goes wrong. Thus, when we break a bone or sprain a ligament, it is during those moments that we count our blessings. When we are, for example, unable to breathe through our nose properly because of a cold, then we remember the great blessing of our health. Being ungrateful is a problem we should attempt to correct. Unfortunately, not only are many of us ungrateful, but we spend our time slamming others over their human imperfections or disabilities.

Imagine how we look in front of Allah ﷻ. There is a proverb that speaks about biting the hand that feeds you; this is exactly what we are doing. Imagine having a young child and feeding that child daily. How ungrateful would it seem if that child, after being fed, then bit your hand? The child, whom you've fed, the provider of the sustenance, has now bitten you. When we make fun of people with physical or intellectual disabilities or insult and harass others, we are disrespecting our Creator and Provider, Allah ﷻ. We benefit from the bodies and minds that Allah ﷻ has given us, yet in turn we mock those of His creations being tested by hardships in their lives. How can we ever imagine growing closer to Allah ﷻ if we belittle and mock His creation?

We should also understand how close ties may be strained because of our tongue. In fact, when Shaytan meets with the shayatin to receive updates on their deceptions, he draws closest to the shaytan who has prompted a husband and wife to argue and break apart. Shaytan knows that when people with close relationships say things in anger or in jest, that they don't really mean, the mark left by those words may forever remain between these individuals. Close relationships bring with them trust and security that allows people not to be on their guard the whole time. But when this trust is violated, people no longer feel safe. This new found vulnerability can lead to further harm. We find in Hadith that the Prophet ﷺ said, "The Muslim is one who other Muslims are safe from his tongue and his hand." (Hadith)

Simply put, Islam attaches great importance to guarding the honour and reputation of others. We should keep in mind that on the Day of Judgment, all of our actions will be judged, especially those that break the rights of others. If the blood of a believer is more dear to Allah ﷻ than His own House (the Ka'bah), think of how much we displease Him if we insult someone whom He loves.

PRACTICAL SOLUTIONS

- Be careful when speaking about people's physical or mental characteristics or attributes.
- Always be grateful for the blessings that you have.
- Speak out against those who mock others – even one person strong enough to speak up can make others realize their mistake.
- Be careful when giving nicknames to friends.
- Remember that if you make fun of a person, then they may in turn make fun of you.
- The Prophet ﷺ neither lied nor did he make a joke at someone else's expense. We should try to avoid telling exaggerated stories and mocking or teasing others just to get a laugh.

Playa' Haterz
Envy & Jealousy

It is human nature to look at others and wish for some of their qualities. We often forget the great characteristics and blessings Allah ﷻ has bestowed upon us and spend our time pining after what we envy in others. Our car may be nice but not as great as someone else's. Or, we may own a pair of Nike shoes but perhaps not the latest ones. Seeing this, we end up feeling bad. We have come to a point where some people are so unhappy with their skin color that they try hard to look like they're from another ethnic group. People will actually pay to darken their skin at a tanning salon or, if they want to appear lighter, they will pay to bleach their skin: it is best though to accept there is nothing wrong with the way we look.

There are various forms of envy, most of which are harmful. Envy falls into these categories: 1) wishing a person who enjoys a blessing will lose it, 2) wishing for a person to lose a blessing while you gain it, 3) wishing that a person will lose a blessing if you cannot attain it yourself, and 4) wishing to have the same blessing as someone else without hoping the other person will lose it. The last type of envy is permissible so long as what you wish to obtain is lawful. Most importantly, you should always say *masha'Allah* (or "what Allah wills") when you see something good that you would like to enjoy the blessing of yourself.

Saying masha'Allah shows you recognize the blessing is a gift from Allah ﷻ. Furthermore, you should also pray that Allah ﷻ increases that person in the particular characteristic you admire and that He blesses you with it as well. Ironically, the selfless act of supplicating for another is actually also personally beneficial. The Prophet ﷺ told us clearly that if a person supplicates for someone else, then the angels in return say *amin* (which is a request that Allah ﷻ answers that supplication) so that the same blessing to given to the person who supplicates.

Similarly beneficial to us is another seemingly selfish act, which is striving to better ourselves and acquire things to help us develop – this can actually be a praiseworthy trait. Having ambition is a characteristic, like many other characteristics we seek to have. When we envy others, we deprive ourselves of potentially greater benefit and veer into harm's way. The desire to better ourselves and to improve, if steered towards improving our souls and bettering our character, can be a path to Jannah. If we look back at our lives and see the amount of effort we put into attaining what others have in this world, we would realize that were even a small portion of that same effort put toward becoming closer to Allah ﷻ, then surely He would have made us more righteous than we are now. Allah ﷻ judges us according to our potential and will never give us something more than what we can handle.

This is beautifully highlighted in various narrations in which some companions would bring an amount to donate for the sake of Allah ﷻ and the Prophet ﷺ would not accept it from them and ask them to donate less, whereas a person like Abu Bakr ؓ donated his entire wealth towards financing the expedition of Tabuk and the Prophet ﷺ accepted it. The reason for this is because various individuals have different capacities for handling difficulties, as Allah ﷻ says:

> *We do not place a burden on a soul except with what it can bear.* (Qur'an 7:42)

We complain we do not have the capability to improve, yet upon real self-examination our abilities will become clear to us. Think of the long nights studying for tests and exams, sometimes sacrificing sleep for nights on end. The goal is to perform to the best of our abilities, and recognizing this, sacrificing whatever is necessary to push ourselves to the limit to achieve success. Sa'ad would relate many stories about himself and his teammates on the wrestling team going for days without eating, or eating very little, in order to make the weight for competitions. Women will starve themselves to fit into a particular outfit for a special occasion. All of these various feats are somehow accomplished which shows our great potential. For those individuals who can stay up all night studying, Allah ﷻ reveals that the same time can be spent praying at night. For those individuals who study, reading chapter upon chapter, Allah ﷻ is showing them they have the ability to read at least a few pages of the Qur'an or from the books of our religion. And for those individuals who can diet for the sake of sport or parties, Allah ﷻ is showing them that they can fast for His sake with ease because their body is able to go certain periods of time without food.

These examples show us we do have the ability to improve, but what we lack is the focus to realize our potential. When we lack this focus and understanding, we fall down the slippery slope of envy because we fail to understand that what others have we can attain too through working hard and applying ourselves. It is at these moments that we begin to ask ourselves why others have something and we do not. At those moments, a jealous pang is driven into our hearts, causing us to feel envy and jealousy for others.

Islam has given us various ways to solve this problem. But before going into those solutions there is an important point we should reflect upon. When we strive to achieve various goals in this world, we want others to be happy for us. It causes pain in our hearts to know that someone may want us to lose what we have worked so hard for. So why would we take it upon ourselves to have such rancour in our hearts for the success of others? What we need to do is put into practice one of the most valuable gifts of the din and that is to pray for such people. It is clear, as we mentioned before, that if a person prays for someone else, the angels say amin to that du'a. Based on other hadith we also know that purity – be it the purity of food, of clothing, of sustenance, and of intention – is an integral part of praying for someone else. Thus, as human beings who undoubtedly commit sins knowingly and unknowingly, we need to work harder to maintain a better state of purity.

If we think of the angels and how pure they are, as creations of Allah ﷻ that cannot disobey Him, it should be very important to seek opportunities for the angels to pray for us. So rather than being envious of someone who has something we want, we should pray for that person. There is a greater likelihood that the prayer of pure beings will be accepted in comparison to the du'as of a person who still needs to improve. So, if we pray that Allah ﷻ grants someone a new car, the angels in turn say amin to that du'a on our behalf, praying to Allah ﷻ that He grant us a new car.

Besides wanting for our brothers and sisters what we would want for ourselves, when we are grateful for what we have already we also keep ourselves from envying others. It comes clearly in the Qur'an,

If you are grateful, verily I will increase you (in it).
(Qur'an 14:7)

The reality is that we already have so much to feel blessed by and contented with in our lives. If we want a new car, the chances are that we already have an older car. Whether or not we get a new car, we need to be genuinely grateful for our current car. If we do not already have a car, we should thank Allah ﷻ for having a bicycle or rollerblades or even for the ability to walk. These are all means of getting around that we have to be grateful for and as a result we may be blessed with the new car we want. The same goes with a home or any other material item. As for those individuals who are jealous of people who are spiritually advanced, the way to better ourselves is to be grateful to Allah ﷻ for whatever advancement in the din we have made. People who feel they are the worst of Muslims should ask for forgiveness and thank Allah ﷻ that at least they are Muslim.

Finally, through spending time with those who are less religious than ourselves and with those who have more than us materially we find changes in ourselves. As a result, we console ourselves that while we are not up to par religiously, we see others who are not even as good as us. And, what is equally as bad is that we begin to desire the material gains and blessings of others who have more than us. This directly contradicts the advice of the Prophet ﷺ. If we are around those who have less than us materially, we will begin to be grateful for what we have and will be less likely to be envious and to want more and more things. Furthermore, if we are around those who are superior to us religiously, we are more likely to notice how much we have to improve ourselves to grow closer to Allah ﷻ.

PRACTICAL SOLUTIONS

- When you see something good say "masha'Allah"; in other words, you should attribute that good thing to Allah.
- When you see someone with a great talent, pray that Allah ﷻ keeps blessing that person and also grants it to you.
- Pray to Allah ﷻ that He protects you from being envious or envied by others through reciting the final three surahs (chapters 112 to 114) of the Qur'an.
- Pray that Allah ﷻ removes any hatred or animosity from your heart.

I Got the Hook Up
Scamming & Cheating

Many people brag about getting clothing, software, CDs, and food at great prices. But we must be very careful not to do something haram like pull a scam that makes for a so-called good story to tell. For example, many of us have friends who work in department retail stores. You go to the store your friend works at, find an item you like, and tell your friend about it. There are two ways your friend can help you get the item. He could use his employment discount and buy it for you. Or, he could charge you for a lower cost item and give you the original. This, my friends, is cheating or even stealing. This is because you did not pay the original price or were not allowed to have the employee discount price. Another example of this is if you have a friend who works at a gas station or convenience store. Your friend tells you to go ahead and pick something up, because the owner has set aside a budget for stolen items, and you do so. These are the ways Shaytan tries to justify evil.

I have seen individuals trying to justify using another person's credit card by stating this is *dar al-harb* (a term meaning "a state of war") and a non-Muslim country so we can cheat people. But there is no justification for stealing from Muslims or non-Muslims. When the Prophet ﷺ was leaving for Madinah and about to make *hijrah*, he left Ali ؓ in Makkah for two reasons. One was so that the Quraysh who were outside his house trying to kill him would think he was still in bed, and in this way Allah ﷻ allowed the Prophet ﷺ to leave safely. Secondly, and more related to the topic, the people of Makkah, Muslims and non-Muslims, had left many of their expensive belongings with the Prophet ﷺ to keep safe, including some of the Quraysh who were arranging to assassinate him. The Prophet ﷺ, despite knowing their devious intentions, still felt he needed to honour the original trusts they had given him by returning their belongings to them. Now that is true piety.

In your life, do those around you operate with such integrity? Students scam on a daily basis at school. But the scamming we see doesn't occur in the cafeteria or bookstore, but in the classroom. But how can that be? After all, there is nothing bought or sold in class. The scamming that we're referring to is of another nature, namely, cheating. We know how difficult life is for a teenager. We have to wake up early in the morning to go to school, spend over eight hours in classes, clubs and practice after school, sometimes work in the evening, and then have hours of homework at night.

Our weekends aren't any better; many of us work at the weekends, and have piles of homework or community service to do – in short, the life of a student isn't as free as everyone makes it out to be. As a result, students don't always have enough time to study and prepare for classes and exams. So when we wake up groggy-eyed in the morning, drag ourselves to school, and get to our first class, the last thing we expect is a quiz. And when it comes, we panic. At this point there is not much hope, despite our frantically skimming through our notes. What's our immediate reaction? For some people, it's to consider cheating.

Cheating is probably the biggest scam and classroom temptation that a student faces. In short, it provides an easy solution to being unprepared, and an individual is rarely caught. What's funny is that the same people who consider stealing from a store or individual as being haram will find themselves cheating in class. The reason for this is that people don't understand the magnitude of this act. It doesn't matter who the person is, cheating seems to plague everyone. It is amazing the excuses cheaters give: "But my friends don't mind that I cheat off them: we all agreed to let each other cheat off one another;" "I'm cheating for the greater good. If I do poorly on this test, my parents will be mad, and it's haram to upset your parents;" "We're cheating to help Islam. If we do well in school we'll get good grades, attend good colleges, and get really good jobs. Then we can donate to Islamic causes and help the Muslims." All of these excuses and most others are unacceptable. But let us take a closer look at cheating so that we can see exactly how harmful this act really is.

There are usually two types of students: those who study and those who do not. The students who study are those who read and study and come prepared for their lessons. As a result, when the time for revision comes they have already prepared themselves and only need to review before their exams. These students prepare themselves properly and are not tempted to cheat. The countless hours of effort and strain go unnoticed as their toil is done behind closed doors.

When test time comes, students who have not studied or put in as much time into studying are worried and decide they need to do something in order to save themselves from performing poorly on the exam. They recognize they made a mistake in not studying and feel they must fix their mistake by making another, which is cheating. They promise themselves not to fall into the same pattern and mistake of not studying again but this habit is so firmly rooted in them that the ease of cheating outweighs the difficulty of studying, causing them to keep on cheating. All the while, in their hearts, some of these cheaters actually even feel their friends were willing to give them their answers to the test. But their friends, who studied hard and put in time and effort preparing, are not always willing to give out the answers.

In fact, the majority of the time they do not want to help in cheating but feel pressurized, feeling that if they don't it will cost them their friendship. In other cases, these poor individuals may be unaware that others are looking over their shoulder and copying down the answers. All the hard work and effort they've put in is being stolen from them without their knowledge. This sharing of knowledge, even if it is with consent, is a kind of theft of intellectual property. By taking intellectual property that is not our own – be it ideas, answers, or anything else – and submitting it as our own work, we are scamming the educational process.

It is funny how when we want a service, we demand the best. Thus, if we hire someone who is incompetent and does not perform their services properly, we complain and demand a discount or a refund. Yet, in our training for various positions we are OK with cheating and claiming for ourselves knowledge that we do not possess. The reality is that we would not want someone servicing our needs who was not properly trained and prepared for the task. If that is the case, we should hold ourselves to the same standard and prepare ourselves properly for whatever comes our way whether it is a test, certification, job interview, or career opportunity. Cheating not only hurts ourselves but has the potential to cause harm to others.

PRACTICAL SOLUTIONS

- If you are getting a deal that is too good to be true, it most likely is.
- Listen to your heart and your conscience.
- Do not cheat in exams.
- Saving a few dollars is not worth the price of a sin.
- If you work at a store or company, please note that you do not own the products or merchandise.
- Remember that Allah ﷻ is watching you, so act like you know that!
- Remember, if you spend the time it would take to make an elaborate plan to cheat in your studies or take short-cuts, then you wouldn't need to cheat in the first place.

Chats, Blogs, Facebook, Oh My!

Internet

Each generation is identified by a certain characteristic. Generation X was the generation of rebellion. Generation Y was the generation whose inquisitive minds led them to question everything. The Mobile or Cell Phone Generation is known by its incessant talking into a machine no matter where they are. Now, inarguably the most fitting name for the current generation of young people is the Internet Generation. Not yet armed with a mobile or cell phone, yet still trying to stay in touch, this generation has tapped into a new method of communication that their seniors are still trying to discover. The internet life of these teens, or rather "professional instant messengers," is quite complex. It is fascinating to watch a teenager simultaneously instant message someone, post on their Xanga, and update their Facebook or Twitter accounts while handling a multi-conversation box screen and three types of messenger at once. This type of performance makes these teens' operation seem truly professional. Yet with these new and awe-inspiring complexities comes a whole new set of problems.

With the advent of Instant Messenger, communication has been taken to an entirely new level. For those who are not aware of how communication has further progressed, imagine that the average youth has nearly 100 buddies on their buddy list. People adjust their conversation box and begin to arrange them along their computer screen so that they are multi-conversing. This scenario sounds essentially harmless but consider the potential hidden dangers.

In the past, it was much easier to distinguish between an appropriate and inappropriate friendship with someone of the opposite gender. Previous generations didn't have computer screens to shield them from the temptations of the opposite sex. Hence not too many of these sisters and brothers got involved in activities that were improper. Nowadays, however, with the Internet often being the most popular method of communication among a younger generation, the variables affecting an average Muslim student's life have changed.

In the past, when a young person wanted to begin talking or getting to know someone of the opposite gender, there was always an embarrassing moment in trying to get a contact for that person. Be it a cell or mobile phone number or a home number, asking for that initial contact information was very awkward. But now, with the spread of instant messaging, youth have a list that at times consist of over 100 people. And then each of these 100 people may have lists of hundreds of more people. Subsequently, this leads to a great opportunity for friends to exchange the names of people from their buddy lists. Now, that awkward moment no longer exists and the obstacle that once prevented youth from stepping into haram has been undermined.

Another temptation that the Internet has made easier is for individuals to manipulate their image. By projecting a more ideal version of ourselves online, we add to our allure whereas in a face-to-face meeting we cannot mask ourselves and the real us is more apparent. A person may have dark hair instead of light, or the wrong eye color, or be too tall or too short for someone else's taste. In the past, when initial contact was initiated through personal meetings, this factor was very important. Now, Instant Messengers, or IMers, are able to alter their image so that they can dress to impress. This isn't through cosmetics or the latest fashion trends; rather, it is through the guise of ever-popular screen names.

Names such as Ali or Aisha may be too dull to impress others, but a name like *longingSOUL* or *cre8ted4U* can be quite appealing. We concoct names that have multiple meanings to attract people. So, *HotHiJABy* says this sister is very good looking *and* that she is religious. Or *Hafiz350z* says this brother is a hafiz who drives a Nissan 350z. A person's physical appearance has been replaced by a really cool screen name. Naturally, even in this technological world, first meetings still leave a long-lasting impression. In the past, people were always nervous about not saying the wrong things, but now instant messaging has taken care of that as well. IM profiles are increasingly popular amongst youth today. A profile allows a different user to learn a little more about a person. But, what is posted on a profile is specifically crafted by posters to attract the right person. Cool pictures, phrases, and lines of poetry are common profiles. "Deep thoughts" or "reflections" are growing as well as they give a glimpse into a person's deeper, more intimate side. But all of these features are just finely crafted measures taken by individuals in order to portray themselves as people they really are not. In fact, most things mentioned on a profile are overstated or greatly understated. Nevertheless, one's identity is not based wholly on reality.

When it comes down to it, many people on Instant Messenger are fake. There is no better way to describe it: they have names that inform yet deceive, profiles that inform yet deceive, and their conversations – unless you regularly speak to the person – usually give you information about a person that is meant to impress and so are in that sense deceptive.

With all of this said, it is important to understand a principle in Islam that is known as *khalwa* (seclusion). Khalwa is the idea of seclusion or being alone and can be beneficial for any believer striving to progress in the din. The Prophet ﷺ himself used to leave the community for long periods of time prior to being blessed with prophethood. In fact, he was given the first revelation while he was secluded in the cave of Hira. But with all good things come bad things. Khalwa can be abused in a manner that motivates Shaytan. For example, the Prophet ﷺ specifically told us how Shaytan will be present in various gatherings. One of those gatherings is a room in which an unrelated man and a woman are seemingly alone, but, in such a coupling, Shaytan is the third party. This is what is taking place in an Instant Messenger box, even though no one else seems to be looking in.

Although a person of the opposite gender is not physically with you, the other elements of privacy are there. The conversation is completely private so no other person is able to view what you are saying. Instant Messenger has advanced to the extent that it allows for the use of a webcam, greetings, emoticons, etc. Such features allow you to express yourself further and to show yourself via pictures or live video streaming. So you can now see the person you are speaking to. All that is left is physical contact with that person, which can be easily arranged through instant messaging. Falling over is imminent once you get on to a slippery slope, unless there is something you can hold on to.

While Internet Messenging and the Internet are not inherently evil, each has the potential to act as a means to do bad deeds. Although this is not our initial intention, the fact of the matter is that much of the Internet does lead towards things that are improper. We should ask ourselves, why is it that we minimize our screens and hide what we are doing when our parents enter the room? Or, we should ask ourselves why is the majority of our activity on the Internet done at night when our parents are asleep while we "stay up late for homework"? Yes, the Internet can be used for many good things. A lot of long lost friends can reconnect with each other and stay in contact through the Internet. But the issue lies more deeply than with the Internet: the issue lies in what our inner self, or nafs, and our desires.

Our nafs is a potential enemy that will either control us or we will control it. The interesting thing about the nafs is that it is one of the few enemies we actually sustain. Feeding or withholding from the nafs is a choice we make, so technically we can cut this enemy off. As a result, Shaytan, our greatest enemy, loses the link he has to us as he can only connect to us through our nafs. But the nafs is a strong force that loves certain things and abhors certain things. Among the things the nafs loves is to waste time and spend it frivolously. Anyone who has spent time on instant messaging knows the majority of the conversations that take place are not vital to our existence. In fact, most of our IM conversations are ways to delay whatever tasks are at hand. As a result, a one-hour homework assignment is delayed by two or three hours. Since wasting time is haram and perhaps even the specific IM conversations we are having are haram as well, we should know the more time we spend in this environment the more potential there is to sin. With the variety of sins now available on the Internet, we should make more of an effort to refrain from the temptations lurking in the virtual world by monitoring how much time is spent and the content of our exchanges.

Bogged with Blogs, Facing off with Facebook, and Finding Myspace

"Dear Diary, you'll never guess what happened today?" Sound familiar? Perhaps most of us have never imagined keeping a diary and for those of us, men or women, who do keep a diary, most would never imagine anyone allowing another person to read this personal tablet of our private thoughts. Yet, we now have Xanga and Blogger. Blogging is taking us by storm. Bloggers are constantly writing about their daily activities, posting random thoughts, or putting up musings in general. Some are very technically savvy and even have interactive audio and video to share with the world. It seems like a harmless tool to record your thoughts and daily events, but when you display yourself intimately this way you are inviting a host of problems into your life.

Today the most popular trend among youth is the use of Facebook and Myspace. As social networking websites, Facebook and Myspace allow participants and members to upload pictures, post their thoughts on blogs, share events, and post thoughts on another person's site that they subscribe to.

In 2009, Facebook and Myspace were ranked as the fourth and the eleventh most popular websites in the world. While these sites have produced the opportunity to meet old friends, advertise Islamic events, and do charitable work, they have a downside. Before we go any further, we are not saying either of these sites are haram. In fact, these websites can be used to do great work. We would just like to direct your attention towards areas that, if avoided, can allow us to save ourselves from harm.

Being mortal, finite beings, we can't live forever so our greatest asset after iman is time. Without time, we will not be able to do good deeds and attain the pleasure of Allah ﷻ. So when we spend our time, we should do so in the wisest way possible. After all, every second we live will not be given back to us until the Day of Judgment, where it will be replayed in front of us and the rest of humanity. Allah ﷻ says in the Qur'an:

> **(I swear)** *By time. Verily mankind is in a state of loss.* (Qur'an 103:1-2)

When people take an oath, they reveal the importance of what they swear by. Which is why, when Muslims take an oath, they often say "Wallahi". In swearing by Allah ﷻ, we show the importance of what we want to say or promise to do. In the verses mentioned above, Allah ﷻ takes an oath by time, showing how important time is. Thereafter, Allah ﷻ makes a statement about humanity that they are in a state of loss. The reason for this is because all humanity is given the time in which to gain the pleasure or wrath of Allah ﷻ. Those who gain the pleasure of Allah ﷻ have used their moments wisely, while those who gain the wrath of Allah ﷻ have misused the time given to them. What is interesting is that Allah ﷻ describes humanity as in a state of loss when it comes to the choice between doing right or wrong at any given moment. But He then follows with the exception:

> *Except for those who believe and do good deeds and exhort one another towards truth and exhort one another towards patience.* (Qur'an 103:3)

For us, as believers, we will gain success through believing, doing good deeds, and motivating others towards the true path and towards being patient. Although this seems like a simple task, this world often diverts our interest from engaging in activities to satisfy this duty. It becomes vital to us as believers to analyze our lives to see what is eating up our time, and take steps toward being more conscious of our actions. For many of us, we spend countless hours on Facebook and Myspace, posting pictures and checking other people's walls, not realizing that we are losing our most valuable asset. As youth, we often ask our bosses for more hours so we can make more money. There will come a time on the Day of Judgment where we will ask Allah ﷻ for more time to do good deeds.

> *Oh my Lord! Send me back in order that I may do righteous deeds in what I neglected.* (Qur'an 23:99-100)

No matter how much a person may plead or beg, Allah ﷻ will respond,

> *By no means! It is but a mere word that he says.*
> (Qur'an 23:100)

Imagine the scene when a person begs Allah ﷻ, having seen the horror of the hellfire, to return to the world and do good deeds. On that day Allah ﷻ will deny everyone that request for they had their opportunity in this world to do good but they did not take advantage of their time.

In addition to wasting precious time, we should be conscious of another factor these sites promote, which is revealing our sins to others. Allah ﷻ, in His infinite mercy, has hidden most of our sins. In previous communities, when a person sinned, their sins were exposed. For some communities in the past, Allah ﷻ would have written the sins on the door of the sinner so that in the morning everyone would see them. For others, if they wanted to repent for their sins, Allah ﷻ would order them:

...so turn in repentance to your Creator and kill yourselves. That is better for you in the sight of your Creator. Verily He is Oft-Returning, the Merciful. (Qur'an 2:54)

But Allah ﷻ, being al-Sattar, has been merciful to the ummah of the Prophet ﷺ. He has chosen for this ummah that, if one commits a sin, then one may repent to Allah ﷻ and seek forgiveness. Allah ﷻ is asking us to be conscious of our actions, to note our mistakes and repent of our sins. Also, the Prophet ﷺ stated that if people hide the sins of others, Allah ﷻ will veil their own sins. If this is the case, then why do Muslims post pictures on Facebook and Myspace that may contain sinful acts being committed by their friends or even themselves? Less obvious perhaps than a photo, the words we type on these portals can also reveal sinful behaviours and thoughts.

When people commit a sin, they often hide it because there is a feeling of shame. This shame is good in that it prevents people from sinning further. If people are trying to hide their sins, it shows that they are still embarrassed of their actions and have the potential of turning back to Allah ﷻ. By feeling shame and embarrassment in front of others, people may eventually find cause to repent to Allah ﷻ. But when people's sins are exposed, they may lose the feeling of shame at being caught and begin to sin openly, no longer feeling the need to hide their sins.

Simply put, new technology can be a means of advancement if used the right way. However, with new technology also comes added responsibility as it allows Shaytan a new inroad to our hearts. So we should be extremely careful to safeguard ourselves from straying away from Allah ﷻ. The last thing we want to do is get stuck in the web Shaytan has spun for us through the World Wide Web.

PRACTICAL SOLUTIONS

- Keep the computer in the kitchen or any other room in the home where people can see what you are doing.
- Be honest with yourself:
  - Which chatrooms are you going to?
  - Who are you talking to?
  - Would you want your parents to see your conversations?
  - What is your real intention when posting on Facebook and or your blog?
  - Who are you posting your pictures for or sending them to?
  - Why are you staying on the internet for so long?
  - How much of your time do you spend on the internet?

The Deadliest Weapon
The Tongue

There is a weapon that has caused more arguments, fights, wars, and personal grudges than any other weapon in the world. This weapon does not make us bleed, but does leave deep psychological wounds. What is scary about this weapon is how freely people use and abuse it. This weapon is so dangerous that Allah ﷻ talks about it in the Qur'an. This weapon is the tongue! It has separated spouses, cousins, siblings, business partners and government leaders, just to name a few. The tongue is so dangerous that when we commit a sin with the tongue, Allah ﷻ will not forgive us until we are forgiven by the individual we talked about or verbally assaulted. The Prophet ﷺ told us that the tongue will 'cause some individuals, who thought they were entering Jannah, to be turned away because all the individuals who they offended will come and surround them in order to take away their good deeds in return for the hurt they felt. Good deeds will be the only currency that will be accepted on that Day of Resurrection.

The tongue has made husbands say things to their wives they wish they hadn't said in the heat of the moment. Teenagers say things to their parents they wish they hadn't said while in a fit of anger. Many young kids have been verbally abused by other kids and parents to the extent that serious emotional and psychological damage has been inflicted. People loose self-esteem and confidence due to the effects of mental torture while growing up and it literally changes whom these people would have become.

The Prophet ﷺ said that if you protect the organs between your jaws and legs you will enter Jannah. Think about this. How many times have one of your friends come up to you and said something like this, "Did you hear about so and so? You don't know what happened? Oh My God! Let me tell you...," or the person says, "You don't know? Okay, forget about it," and you say "No, come on, tell me, I won't tell anyone, you can trust me, wallahi." Sound familiar? The Prophet ﷺ reminded us that both parties in this case are sinful: the one who gossips and the one who listens to gossip. The listener enables the other to gossip and backbite, so both are at fault.

We need to be very careful when we talk about others. Not only is gossip haram if it is true but it is made even worse when the conversation is based on suspicion and assumption. Let's be honest, in the Muslim community words travel fast. For example, if the gossip is about a girl and unnecessary information about her is passed on from one person to another then this has great potential to damage her reputation. Gossiping about others not only ruins reputations, but it can also hurt feelings, break up relationships, and cause damage to whole communities, and not just individuals.

The tongue also gets us in trouble by our everyday language, especially swearing and cussing. Many times when we are talking to our friends we use terms like the f-word or the s-word like it isn't anything bad. While our environment may influence us, it is not a valid excuse. There is no justification for this. We are people who only call people by the best of names, names that they are happy to hear. In fact, the Prophet ﷺ said that the one who curses is not from amongst us. Teenagers especially need to be very careful about their language as they are looked up to by younger children. Kids mimic everything teenagers do and will begin swearing if exposed to it by those they admire. The scary thing is that if they learn a bad word because they heard it from you, every time they say that word you also get a sin until the day they die! Ask yourself if one of your friends, siblings, or classmates has learned a swear word from you. Do you really want to have that on your shoulders? But look at the flip side: if you teach them something good like a surah, as-salam 'alaykum, some dhikr or good manners, then every time this person uses this knowledge and gets a good deed you will also be rewarded with a good deed until they pass away.

This tongue that Allah ﷻ has created is so small and delicate yet it is a muscle that never tires. While we can exercise our arms and legs until they tire out and are no longer able to lift a pound, the tongue can be used continuously without ever needing a rest. In understanding the power of the tongue, we need to keep in mind that we can use it to attain the pleasure of Allah ﷻ, the highest rank in this world or the hereafter, or we can use it to destroy ourselves.

> *On the Day when their tongues, their hands, and their feet will bear witness against them as to what they did.*
> (Qur'an 24:24)

We have to ask ourselves, "from which group do we want to be?"

PRACTICAL SOLUTIONS

- If you're not going to say something good, then don't say anything at all.
- If you know someone is backbiting about someone else to you, try changing the subject or explaining to that person why it's not good to backbite – or at least walk away.
- If you are angry with someone, it is best to leave the room; the majority of the time you will regret later on what you will say in anger.
- Do not listen to music that has swearing in its lyrics as you will be more likely to swear.
- Be conscious of your environment – which includes the people you hang out with and where you are – as it will often affect what you're going to say or how you're going to say it.
- Try to get your tongue used to doing dhikr and reading the Qur'an as the tongue cannot say two things at once.
- Pray that Allah ﷻ moistens your tongue with His remembrance and fill your ears with the remembrance of Allah ﷻ.

Fantasy World
Pornography

When we began writing this book, there were a few topics we weren't sure we should include. Amongst them was this chapter on pornography. In our culture and society, this problem is rampant, but it is rarely spoken about. This is a topic that many individuals are embarrassed to talk about, but it is a growing epidemic in and outside of our community. With the growing access to pornography online, it has risen to become a $97 billion business worldwide, with the US and the UK having 14% and 2% of the market in 2006. In fact, the pornography industry is larger than the revenues of the top technology companies – Microsoft, Google, Amazon, eBay, Yahoo!, Apple, Netflix, and EarthLink – combined. The US pornography revenue exceeded the combined revenues of ABC, CBS, and NBC!

This problem has been rapidly growing in our community and has been something that we have continuously tried to hide. The matter remains that more and more people are now accessing pornography for their own pleasure, but most people do not understand how destructive this can be. Just look at the startling statistics about pornography:

- Every second – $3,075.64 is being spent on pornography
- Every second – 28,258 Internet users are viewing pornography
- Every second – 372 Internet users are typing adult search terms into search engines
- Every 39 minutes – a new pornographic video is being created in the United States

What is more shocking is looking at these statistics about children and teenagers and pornography:

- Average age of first Internet exposure to pornography: 11 years old
- 15-17 year olds having multiple exposure to hard-core pornography: 80%
- 8-16 year olds having viewed porn online: 90% (most while doing homework)
- 7-17 year olds who would freely give out home address: 29%
- Children's character names linked to thousands of porn links: 26 (including Pokemon and Action Man)

What we should all understand that, once this habit starts, it is hard to stop. These images are stored in our memory and Shaytan brings them out at times when we are alone. Just as we spoke about in the chapter on "Lowering Your Gaze," a believer is not permitted to look at the opposite gender clothed, and the rulings are even stricter when a person is unclothed. Furthermore, acts of intimacy between husband and wife are meant to be kept private.

Another problem that also arises from pornography is that such material gives people wrong expectations. Pornography, like all media, is scripted. Individuals who watch pornography become accustomed to what they see. As a result, they not only have unrealistic expectations of how their spouse should look, but they also feel that their marriage is lacking or flawed if their intimacy with their spouse does not reach that scripted ideal. This can be extremely detrimental to individuals as well as marriages because people can have serious issues of self-esteem: if they feel they have not matched up to some false ideal, then they begin to compare themselves, their spouse, and their marriage to something that is staged. Many marriages have fallen apart because people are unable to differentiate between reality and acting.

As Muslims, we are not immune from this either. In a report showing the 2006 Search Engine Request Keyword Trend, eight out of ten of the top worldwide leaders in search requests for the word "sex" were Muslim countries. We have to face the reality that Muslims are being affected by this as well. The question is: how do we stop it?

2006 Search Engine Request Keyword Trends	
Top Worldwide Search Requests	Top US Cities Search Requests
Keyword: "porn"	
1. South Africa	1. Elmhurst, IL
2. Ireland	2. Stockton, CA
3. New Zealand	3. Meriden, CT
4. United Kingdom	4. Chandler, AZ
5. Australia	5. Louisville, KY
6. Estonia	6. Irvine, CA
7. Norway	7. Kansas City, KS
8. Canada	8. Norfolk, VA
9. Croatia	9. Tampa, FL
10. Lithuania	10. Oklahoma City, OK
Keyword: "xxx"	
1. Bolivia	1. Elmhurst, IL
2. Chile	2. Meriden, CT
3. Romania	3. Oklahoma City, OK
4. Ecuador	4. Irvine, CA
5. Pakistan	5. Kansas City, KS
6. Peru	6. Tampa, FL
7. Mexico	7. Chandler, AZ
8. Slovenia	8. Norfolk, VA
9. Lithuania	9. Richardson, TX
10. Colombia	10. Las Vegas, NV
Keyword: "sex"	
1. Pakistan	1. Elmhurst, IL
2. India	2. Meriden, CT
3. Egypt	3. Kansas City, KS
4. Turkey	4. Louisville, KY
5. Algeria	5. Southfield, MI
6. Morocco	6. Newark, NJ
7. Indonesia	7. Oklahoma City, OK
8. Vietnam	8. Norfolk, VA
9. Iran	9. Irvine, CA
10. Croatia	10. Chandler, AZ

If the average age of first exposure to pornography is 11, it becomes clear to us that this is no longer a problem restricted to adults. Thus, it becomes important to realize its effects. Initially, a person who becomes exposed to pornography will naturally begin to become addicted to it and will want to see more. Many people feel that they can stop this act whenever they want, especially after marriage, but most of the complaints that we get are from married people who find out that their spouses are addicted to pornography. As children are exposed and become addicted to this habit, they begin to fantasize about sex. These individuals are then put in a difficult situation where all of these feelings and desires are burning them up inside and they need an outlet. Many other sins result from watching pornography as the initial sight turns into desire and eventually into action. The results are mind boggling. In high school, one out of every four teenagers has a sexually-transmitted disease (STD). Teenage pregnancy and birth rates in the United States (over a third) and in Britain (over a quarter) are the highest in the western world between the ages of 15 and 19.

What is worse is that some youth have become used to what they have seen and want something new. They begin to search for new genres of pornography, things that would never have been thought of before. Furthermore, these thoughts also lead men in particular to degrade women, painting them as only objects of desire. The sad state of affairs in our community is that abuse is on the rise. When we do things that allow us to see our women as objects rather than human beings, we are creating an environment in which we neither respect our women nor set a good example for our families. It becomes clear here why the Prophet ﷺ had put "guarding what is between the two legs" as one of the means to attaining Jannah.

Allah ﷻ knows and the Prophet ﷺ knew that we have these natural desires within us. The Prophet ﷺ advised young men, if possible, to marry at a young age. Allah ﷻ ordered believing men and women to lower their gazes, and for women to cover themselves. Furthermore, as we mentioned earlier, Allah ﷻ ordered the believers not to come close to fornication.

And do not come close to fornication. (17:32)

By the eyes seeing the images that are in magazines, videos, and sites, the hearts will have these images embedded within them, paving a road to travel down until fornication is reached. We cannot fool ourselves into thinking that what we are doing is not serious and is not paving the way to fornication: "The eyes, their fornication is an illicit sight." (Hadith)

The idea is for us to understand that this is wrong, and although this may be difficult for us to overcome, we can do so by making a clear intention and working hard to give up this habit. It may be difficult initially, and we may stumble and fall. Be realistic, and set a timetable. Set a goal for a few days or a week. Try to reach that goal and mark it on a secret calendar that no one else sees. Put black crosses for the days that we are able to stay away from it and red crosses for the days that we stumble. After reaching the target of a week, then set the goal for two weeks, then a month, and build on it. Allah ﷻ will see our intentions and reward us for it with strength and support. We should remember that if we repent and refrain from such actions, then we give ourselves the opportunity to attract the mercy and blessings of Allah ﷻ.

PRACTICAL SOLUTIONS

- Your computer should not be in your bedroom.
- You should not be surfing the web alone, especially late at night.
- You should buy a cyber patrol program that has filters. Buy it and have your parents set the password so you don't know what it is. This way you will not be tempted to unlock the filter yourself.
  - Make sure when you get an email or a pop-up to read before you click, once you get in, it is tough to get out. Companies have researched this and purposefully give free tours.

- Pray that Allah protects you from the whispers of Shaytan.
- Ask forgiveness from Allah ﷻ if you've looked at something you shouldn't have, and pray that Allah ﷻ protects you from seeing anything that is harmful for you.

General Statistics:

Internet Pornography Statistics	
Pornographic websites	4.2 million (12% of total websites)
Pornographic pages	420 million
Daily pornographic search engine requests	68 million (25% of total search engine requests)
Daily pornographic emails	2.5 billion (8% of total emails)
Internet users who view porn	42.7%
Received unwanted exposure to sexual material	34%
Average daily pornographic emails/user	4.5 per Internet user
Monthly Pornographic downloads (peer-to-peer)	1.5 billion (35% of all downloads)
Daily Gnutella "child pornography" requests	116,000
Websites offering illegal child pornography	100,000
Sexual solicitations of youth made in chat rooms	89%
Youths who received sexual solicitation	1 in 7 (down from 2003 statistic of 1 in 3)
Worldwide visitors to pornographic web sites	72 million visitors to pornography: Monthly
Internet Pornography Sales	$4.9 billion

Adult Internet Pornography Statistics	
Men admitting to accessing pornography at work	20%
US adults who regularly visit Internet pornography websites	40 million
Promise Keeper men who viewed pornography in last week	53%
Christians who said pornography is a major problem in the home	47%
Adults admitting to Internet sexual addiction	10%
Breakdown of male/female visitors to pornography sites	72% male – 28% female

Women and Pornography	
Women keeping their cyber activities secret	70%
Women struggling with pornography addiction	17%
Ratio of women to men favoring chat rooms	2X
Percentage of visitors to adult websites who are women	1 in 3 visitors
Women accessing adult websites each month	9.4 million
Women admitting to accessing pornography at work	13%

Statistics from www.familysafemedia.com

I Can't Fight This Feeling Anymore
Suicide, Depression & Abuse

Life is hard. There's really no other way to put it – life is hard. Allah ﷻ addresses this clearly,

> *Or do you think you will enter into Heaven [with ease]?*
> (Qur'an 2:214)

This verse specifically poses the question for people to under-stand that entering Jannah is not possible without various difficulties surrounding it. Sometimes the difficulties are minor, and, with a few comforting words from friends, we are able to overcome them. However, sometimes the tests are so difficult we begin to question ourselves, our faith, and life in general. These tests are dangerous because they shake us to such an extent that we want to give up. But this is the path that we tread as believers. The Sahabah had difficult lives, having to go most of their lives living in poverty, staying on guard to defend against enemy attacks, and watching their loved ones being tortured and killed. Even our Prophet ﷺ had to undergo great difficulty.

Look at the life of our Prophet ﷺ. Imagine the difficulties that were laid down on the path he walked on. Imagine not knowing who our father was, not seeing our mother after the age of six, or having our grandfather as our guardian and then watching him pass away. Then imagine growing up in poverty, only to marry a beautiful, wealthy spouse, and then having to watch that spouse pass away from the weakness attained from being boycotted for following our message. Imagine seeing five of our children passing away and our friends being tortured for believing in our message. This is only the tip of the iceberg of what the Prophet ﷺ used to go through. Despite this fact, he remained pleased in serving his Creator. In him lies the greatest example for us,

> **Verily in the Messenger of Allah is the greatest example for you.** (Qur'an 33:21)

Depression

"I'm all alone," "No one understands me," "This medicine isn't gonna fix how I feel," "They keep telling me its all in my head," "Things would be better if I wasn't here," "How is talking to someone gonna help."

These are a few of the feelings that people have had at some point in their life. It is normal to feel upset or down when we experience a tragedy in our lives such as death, divorce, and other major changes. Clinical depression has a certain number of required symptoms in order for one to be diagnosed with it – that's up to a psychiatrist to decide. We're not here to tell anyone to go see one, but we do want to let everyone know that "you are not alone!"

Having depression is very difficult. It is an illness like diabetes or hypertension, and like these illnesses, it also can be treated. Many people in today's society don't think of depression as an illness and instead label depressed people as unable to control themselves or their feelings or think they are just "crazy". But in reality it *is* a treatable disease. When people have high blood pressure they are not just sent home with medication and told to continue everything they were doing before. They are told to change things in their life to help. The same holds true for depression. Medication alone won't cure most people. Rather, a person may need to see a therapist, a therapy group, or other multidisciplinary options.

When it comes to depression, the feeling of hopelessness is the loneliest feeling anyone can feel. A person will no longer have the desire to do anything or be with anyone. Some people when they're at the bottom of the barrel think that no one else could feel any worse. This never-ending cascade of feelings is what most depressed people experience. But that feeling and its effects touch everyone. Family members get affected by this illness as well because a change in us affects them as well. And by not wanting to be around them or do anything with them can often make matters worse. Not only does a person feel worthless, but they feel bad that they are making others upset in the process. It is complicated. Trying to make sense of it can at times make a person feel helpless.

What also hurts someone in this situation is that there is a stigma, unfortunately, attached to people who suffer from depression. Our community tends to shun them and look down upon their taking medication. The reality is that we need to begin to push past such stupidity and start realizing that we are being effected by these problems. And, in order for us to be a successful community, we will have to take these situations seriously. With that being said, we should not turn away from seeing a therapist or psychiatrist if necessary. We've seen many uncles not go to see a heart doctor because they wanted to continue eating *biriyani* or other favorite foods. The end result is that they damage their bodies to such an extent that they have made life difficult for themselves and others who subsequently have to take care of them. Rather, if they had seen a doctor, they could have changed their diet or taken exercise, and they would have found their lives more enjoyable and easier to live. The same goes for depression. Yes, no one likes to take medication and no one would like to have to undergo therapy. However, Allah ﷻ mentions in the Qur'an,

> *And it is possible that you may dislike a thing and it is better for you, and it is possible that you may like a thing but it is harmful for you.* (Qur'an 2:216)

While we might prefer to keep away from medication or seeking professional help, that help may be what is necessary for us in order to draw us closer to Allah ﷻ.

There is also a spiritual element to depression. Allah ﷻ has created everything in a balance and has advised us not to break that balance,

And do not ruin the balance. (Qur'an 55:9)

Not only was nature made in a perfect balance, but even humans have been made with a balance. There are two components that make up our existence, the soul and the body, and one cannot exist without the other. The body has been created from the earth, and it derives nourishment from it; the soul, on the other hand, was created in the heavens, and takes its nourishment from the heavens in the form of prayer, fasting, charity, etc.

As long as the soul and body are fed in balance, they will remain in a good state. However, when the body is overly-fed with the things of this world and the focus is no longer on Allah ﷻ, then that is when depression can kick in. The body begins to take in fewer prayers, fasts, charity, and ends up taking in the joys and pleasures of this world. Thus, the body is stimulated by the soul and becomes depressed.

The solution for this depression is fairly simple. We need to always monitor what we are consuming. By consuming, we don't mean only eating, but taking anything in. For example, people who want to nourish their bodies do not necessarily have to only eat. Rather, they can be nourished through other means such as intravenous drips. Similarly, we can also feed our souls in various ways. If we look at things that are rewarding, such as a page of the Qur'an, our parents with love, and so on, then these actions would feed our souls positively. Furthermore, we can feed ours souls by listening to Qur'an or lectures on Islam. With this in mind, in order to avoid spiritual depression, we watch our various inputs and see what is entering our body. In Ramadan, what's interesting is that we reduce our bodily input by not eating, drinking or having marital relations from dawn to sunset, yet we grow accustomed to it. Furthermore, we increase our spiritual input by praying more, reading the Qur'an more, and generally increasing our acts of worship. By the end of

Ramadan, we experience the opposite of depression: we are elated through our closeness to Allah ﷻ. Praying is an entirely new experience, and the Qur'an has new depths for us. All of this is in the middle of our basically starving ourselves. Why? Because while we have decreased our earthly inputs, we have increased our heavenly inputs, which results in elation. When we make the mistake of increasing our earthly inputs and decreasing our heavenly and spiritual inputs, we can begin to feel depressed. Whether the depression we are undergoing is hereditary, learned behaviour or through spiritual weakness, we always need to remember that this test has come from Allah ﷻ. Allah ﷻ even tells us to look at the life of Prophet Ayub ﷺ,

And remember our servant, Ayub. (Qur'an 38:41)

Here is a prophet whom Allah ﷻ describes as being a grateful slave. What was it about Prophet Ayub ﷺ that made him so grateful? When looking at his life we see initially a man who was showered with the blessings of Allah ﷻ. He was constantly in the obedience of Allah ﷻ and was grateful for all the various blessings given to him. Shaytan, as a result, complained to Allah ﷻ claiming that Prophet Ayub ﷺ was only being grateful because of the various blessings he had been given. So in order to display to Shaytan how great of a servant Prophet Ayub ﷺ was, Allah ﷻ granted Shaytan the power to test Prophet Ayub, knowing his servant would be grateful. One by one, Allah ﷻ permitted Shaytan to take away various blessings from his wealth, children and family, and his own health. Every time a blessing was taken away, Shaytan would claim that Prophet Ayub ﷺ was remaining patient because of other blessings he still received. In order to further try to mislead Prophet Ayub ﷺ, Shaytan would come disguised and question the Prophet Ayub ﷺ as to why he was still worshipping Allah ﷻ when he was being mistreated to such an extent. Prophet Ayub ﷺ would continuously cite, for example, that he was given so many years of health, should he not be grateful for it and be patient in this short time of difficulty.

We may not understand the severity of his tests. It comes in one narration that when Prophet Ayub's children were taken from him, the manner in which they were taken was the roof of their home collapsed. Such was the weight of the roof collapsing that when Shaytan approached Prophet Ayub ﷺ to describe the scene, he specifically mentioned seeing one of his sons having his head crushed and his brain having come from his nose. In another narration, it was mentioned that his entire body became infected with wounds and in those wounds worms and other insects began to grow and feed. Yet, despite these difficulties, he persevered, remained patient, and did not allow for it to be a means of turning away from Allah ﷺ. As a result, he was given back everything and more as he had remained patient and passed his test,

> *And We gave him back his family and the like of them with them, as a mercy from Us, and as a reminder for those who posses understanding.* (Qur'an 38:43)

Most importantly, however, he received a stamp of approval from Allah ﷺ as he was described in the Qur'an,

> *Truly We found him patient. How excellent a slave! Verily he was oft-returning in repentance to Us.* (Qur'an 38:44)

Suicide

It can seem like it's the easiest option. In fact, sometimes it seems like it's the only way out. After all, when all else fails, what else can a person do? However, while the solution may seem simple but it is much more serious than we can imagine. In the end, we have to make sure we never fall into despair.

The major mistake of Iblis was actually that he despaired of the mercy of Allah ﷺ. We are told specifically in the Qur'an,

> *Do not despair of the mercy of Allah. Indeed Allah forgives all sins.* (Qur'an 39:53)

Rather than turning back, as we mentioned before, in repentance to Allah ﷻ, Iblis despaired. That error is what we need to be weary of. After all, any complication or difficulty in our lives is from Allah ﷻ as a test or a punishment. Both are glad tidings for a believer. If it's a test, then we can earn reward from Allah ﷻ by being patient and subsequently attain a higher position in the eyes of Allah ﷻ. And, if it's a punishment, then we are being given a smaller punishment in this world and will be saved from a greater punishment in the hereafter.

Also, if we are being tested or punished by Allah ﷻ, then we should also not despair as Allah ﷻ says clearly in the Qur'an,

Allah does not place a burden on a soul greater than what it can handle. (Qur'an 2:286)

This is an immense blessing of Allah ﷻ for, even though it is within His right to test us as much as He wills, He will never test us more than what we can handle. As a result, what we initially need to realize is that the point of a test is to try us. It may at times bring us to the brink, but it will never be more than we can handle because Allah ﷻ has guaranteed us that.

Given that, it should also be mentioned that the initial feelings a person experiences from a test will be challenging. In fact, the anxiety faced will often test a person's mettle. Sometimes after the initial test, things become easier. But sometimes things will actually get worse. We all do wish that there always was an easy solution to overcome a difficulty. But, unfortunately, that isn't always the case. One thing we recommend is to reflect on the previous occasions that a difficult situation arose. At that point we all thought that our lives would get worse and we would never be able to recover from it. However, years later, when we look back at the entire fiasco, we are often able to laugh at ourselves. The reason is simple: this world is temporary, and so are its trials and tests. So the only mistake we can make is trying to solve a temporary difficulty with a permanent solution.

Suicide is the act of taking one's own life intentionally. For people who feel that life has brought them to a point of no return, suicide inevitably seems like the only escape. As a result, people end up taking their own lives, thinking that they will not have to worry about any repercussions, only to find out that the hereafter and its punishments are real and permanent. Suicide is impermissible in Islam. Allah ﷻ says regarding it,

And do not kill yourselves. (Qur'an 4:29)

Furthermore, the punishment has been highlighted repeatedly in Hadith: "Whoever purposely throws himself from a mountain and kills himself, will be in the Fire, falling down into it and abiding therein perpetually forever; and whoever drinks poison and kills himself with it, he will be carrying his poison in his hand and drinking it in the Fire, wherein he will abide eternally forever; and whoever kills himself with an iron weapon, will be carrying that weapon in his hand and stabbing his abdomen with it in the Fire, wherein he will abide eternally forever." (Hadith)

The punishments of the Fire, even though we might think of a worldly equivalent, will be infinitely worse. So while repeated suicide may include the pain of the act and the horrors of death, those pains will be increased many times in the hellfire. Now what seemed like an easy getaway has resulted in being a terrible punishment.

Our purpose here isn't to scare anyone. Many of us have, probably, at one point or another wished we could solve our problems by ending it all. But the affair of a believer is a very strange one, as every situation has benefit in it. In fact, regarding desiring death, the Prophet Muhammad ﷺ said, "None amongst you should make a request for death, and do not call for it before it comes, for when any of you dies, he ceases (to do good) deeds and the life of a believer is not prolonged but for goodness." (Hadith)

For the believer, life is a tool to attain Jannah. When Allah ﷻ feels that a believer will no longer benefit from life, He ends that person's life as He doesn't want that person to be harmed by further mistakes. Having that faith in Allah ﷻ is necessary so that we can have faith that He is not going to harm us in any way, which should comfort us in our stressful moments. Some scholars mention that when the Prophet Muhammad ﷺ was initially given revelation, the responsibility was so heavy and so difficult to carry that he contemplated ending his life. However, he remained patient and steadfast, and, as a result, he was tested even more. But the principle is simple: Allah ﷻ only tests those whom He loves. That's why we find the prophets going through the most difficult tests to a point that,

> *Until the prophet and those with him said "Where is the help of Allah?"* (Qur'an 2:214)

This was even highlighted by the Prophet ﷺ when he said, "The most severe tests are for the prophets, then those closest to them, then those closest to them." (Hadith) But there's light at the end of the tunnel. They did not allow these tests to overwhelm them, Allah ﷻ responded to their call of need for

> *Verily the help of Allah is near.* (Qur'an 2:214)

Abuse

As a community, we may want to ignore the fact that abuse is prevalent in our society. It is a growing sickness in our community, which claims new victims daily. With each case of abuse, the victim becomes more and more demoralized until they, like most victims, begin to blame themselves for being abused. Both the perpetrators and the victims are unaware of the lasting effects of abuse. Simply put, abuse is the exploitation of an individual through physical or psychological mistreatment. This exploitation can have a variety of aspects, and can even be, at times, done unconsciously. That's why it becomes extremely important to recognize what is abuse and to learn how to see the signs and symptoms of abuse so that we may help others who are being abused.

To begin with it is important to state that we understand that victims of abuse may feel they deserve this treatment. So this mindset of so-called deserving victimization has to be addressed immediately. We should remember that Allah 🕮 has not created mankind in a debased state; rather He says:

And verily we honoured the children of Adam. (Qur'an 17:70)

Our responsibility in this world is to serve Him and grow closer to Him through our service. Part of that service is to be good to others. The Prophet Muhammad 🕮 said about himself and his role upon humanity, "Verily I have been sent to perfect moral character." (Hadith)

Furthermore, Allah 🕮 himself testifies to the truth of this,

Verily you possess an exalted character. (Qur'an 69:4)

As members of the ummah of the Prophet 🕮, it is our ongoing responsibility to serve others and to make life easier for everyone. Given this, it is easy to see that abuse is not a part of the din.

In fact, Anas 🕮, a young companion who from a young age served the Prophet 🕮 for ten years, said that the Prophet 🕮 never once rebuked or yelled at him. The accounts of many other companions besides Anas's show the mercy of the Prophet Muhammad 🕮 towards his followers. The Prophet 🕮 never abused anyone, including prisoners of war. In fact, it is the case that many non-Muslims became Muslim after they were well-treated, even as prisoners of war.

There are various reasons as to why people abuse others. After speaking to a few psychologists, it became increasingly apparent that abuse occurs in a cycle. Although this is not a reason to excuse abuse, it is important to understand that many people who were abused when they were younger then subsequently abuse others when they became adults.

If we have been or are victims of abuse, we need to take the proper steps to make sure we don't fall into the same cycle of abusing others.

Physical and verbal abuse has grown rapidly in our ummah. For various reasons, whether to vent anger, to show their superiority, to hold on to some delusion of power, many men in our community, and some women, have become increasingly physically abusive. This is something the Prophet ﷺ never did. It is mentioned that "The Prophet never beat any of his wives or servants; in fact, he did not strike any living being with his hand except in the cause of Allah or when the prohibitions of Allah had been violated, and he retaliated on behalf of Allah." (Hadith) In fact, he said very clearly that "abusing a Muslim is a sin". (Hadith) This very clear guidance can be misunderstood or ignored by parents, guardians and teachers. As a result, it is necessary to clarify repeatedly that a person should never rebuke their children or students. In general, if someone feels that physical action is necessary, our scholars cite lessons from the sunnah to give us guidelines on how to reprimand someone.

The idea of mercy is prevalent in the sunnah. 'A'ishah ﵁ mentioned that, "A bedouin came to the Prophet ﷺ and asked, 'Do you kiss your children? We do not kiss them.' The Prophet ﷺ said, 'Can I put mercy in your hearts after Allah has removed it from them?'" (Hadith) In another narration it is stated, "The Messenger of Allah ﷺ kissed Hasan ibn 'Ali while al-Aqra' ibn Habis at-Tamimi was sitting with him. Al-Aqra' observed, 'I have ten children and I have not kissed any of them.' The Messenger of Allah ﷺ looked at him and said, 'Whoever does not show mercy will not be shown mercy.'" (Hadith) These stories show how our Messenger ﷺ preached and acted with children. He also made it clear that those who do not show mercy to their young will never be shown mercy or respect themselves.

This also applies to husbands and wives. Spousal abuse is on the rise in our communities. It is so embarassing to know that some men have digressed so far from the teachings of Islam that they would raise a hand at their wives and then say that they have a right to beat their wives. This is ridiculous! The previous hadith mentions clearly that the walking Qur'an himself never hit a woman! The Prophet ﷺ taught that, "The best of you are those who are best to their families (wives). And I am the best towards my families (wives)." (Hadith) He also mentioned that, "The believers who show the most perfect faith are those who have the best behavior, and the best of you are those who are best to their wives." (Hadith)

Teachings like these completely refute the terrible concept of co-called honour killing and other ignorant ideas that people have brought into the din. We have to honour our children and spouses, both men and women. Islam came to remove the ways of *jahilliyah* (pre-Islamic ignorance), including womanizing and burying daughters alive. However, while we may not physically bury our daughters alive anymore, we have begun to bury them alive in other ways.

It's difficult to write this, but it's necessary. What has happened to the Muslim ummah? Have we forgotten about our Lord so much that we have turned to heinous acts like sexual or physical abuse? As a community, we may want to pretend that it doesn't exist, but the reality is that awareness of this problem is growing. For those who are reading this and are doing this, stop this act now. No one understands the magnitude of this, but when we have had to sit down with these individuals and see the way it has affected them, their families, and their marriages, it is heartbreaking. For the victims of this horrific act, please remember the following.

Never think it's your fault! Victims often begin to think that they asked for it. That can never be true. Understand that this is the sin of the perpetrator and not your fault at all. Also, you must seek help. This type of abuse can destroy lives. Victims sometimes seek acceptance or security, so they begin to loose their sense of boundaries. For example, they become so affected that they cannot be close to anyone, including their spouses. This can affect either men or women. Help is available in various forms. As a community, we need to break free from the stigma of the victim as dishonoured. Be it a comment, a touch, or even rape, the victim is not at fault and should not be treated as morally suspect. They should be supported and cared for by the community and given the opportunity to see a therapist to begin the healing process. The worst thing that can happen, which is something that we've both seen is, is that parents blame the child or try to convince the child that nothing has happened. We have parents who would rather protect the honour of the victimizer rather than caring for the wellbeing of the victim. Much of it has to do with the abuse having occurred regularly overseas and never having been addressed. What makes this worse is that so-called respectable members of our community have become involved in this. That makes the victims feel that they are at fault.

Everyone needs to become aware of this problem and see that it is completely impermissible. In fact, all the verses that refer to guarding the gaze even apply to young children. This is because sometimes Shaytan can whisper into the hearts and cause desire to become manifest. This doesn't mean we cannot look at children. Rather, it means we have to be vigilant and careful in our interactions with children. We should always be careful never to be alone with someone about whom Shaytan has whispered something into our hearts. The reason is to forestall any danger and to protect these children from any possible harm or abuse. We constantly hear about religious officials from various faiths that have molested children. Why do we feel this won't affect Muslims? Ibn al-Jawzi ﷺ mentions there are several hadith that forbid looking at children with lustful gazes. This shows that this problem or the potential of this problem has existed in the past. If any of us are involved in this, we need to repent to Allah ﷻ and seek His forgiveness and guidance.

This world can be a cruel place, but, just remember, never give up hope. Every test is a means of purification and elevation. So, if there are victims reading this, know that even though it seems tragic and unfair to have gone through this horrific problem, there are always ways to get help and to see redress. Ultimately, as believers, we should remember that any trial, however horrendous, is temporary, and the reward given in the hereafter is permanent. And in heaven, there is no feeling of pain or sorrow, only an unending feeling of bliss and happiness.

PRACTICAL SOLUTIONS

- Remember that Allah ﷻ wil not burden us with more than we can bear.
- Ask Allah ﷻ for patience.
- Read Qur'an and do dhikr for comfort.
- Speak to a trusted friend for advice.
- Never blame yourself for being victimized.
- Do not be afraid to confront or have someone you trust confront the victimizer.
- Speak to a suitably-qualified and sympathetic imam or professional counselor about the situation in order to receive proper help, therapy, and treatment.
- Exercise or do physical activity. With depression, our levels of serotonin, a chemical neuro-transmitter than regulates appetite, mood and anger, go down; exercise helps keep those levels up.
- Victimizers and victims should know and understand that there is never any justification for any type of abuse.

Part 2: **Solutions**

The Bestseller from the Greatest Author

Qur'an

We often hear the cliché: an apple a day keeps the doctor away. And just as our physical selves need a preventative and good balance of nourishment to stay healthy, our spiritual selves also need exactly the same thing. In this regard, a page a day keeps the Shaytan away. The Qur'an is our book of guidance, and we need to get acquainted with our Holy Book. One of the greatest things we can do for our spiritual betterment is to start reciting the Qur'an in Arabic as well as reading it in English. Even if one does not understand the meaning of the Arabic, there is still a great reward in reciting the Qur'an. For each letter a person recites, there is ten times the reward. How many people do you know who have memorized an entire Shakespearean play, a Harry Potter book, or even the Bible? This is the only book in history that people have taken years to memorize and preserve it in its entirety. This is the only book that is recited by millions of people everyday. Think about how many times you have focused for four to six hours studying for a science or humanities test. How many of us have focused that much time on the book authored by the Creator of the Universe? The Prophet ﷺ advised us to do any good act and to do it consistently, "The most beloved actions to Allah are those that are consistent, even if little." (Hadith) Even reciting a page of the Qur'an a day, which with practice only takes a few minutes, is a rewarded act blessed by Allah ﷻ.

Some of us may have a difficult time reciting it in Arabic, but even for that person there is an incentive. The Prophet ﷺ has told us that the reward for the individual who struggles to recite the Qur'an will be twice as much. In a normal classroom, a teacher doesn't normally reward a student for struggling to read; the teacher may even be disappointed with that child. But our fear and worries about reciting the Qur'an are all from Shaytan and we should not let Shaytan feed us with excuses such as it being too late to start learning how to recite the Qur'an or that it will be embarrassing to learn when we have passed a certain age. "What if people find out?" If that is our worry, then we should pick an individual whom we are comfortable with and ask that person to help us. Many people will be glad to assist as it is an investment of a lifetime for them.

Allah ﷻ will reward each and every individual uniquely, for He knows the path each of us tread in order to get closer to Him. If our parents did not teach us to recite the Qur'an or did not tell us about Islam and we are struggling on our own, we should find respite in the fact that Allah ﷻ is al-'Alim (All-Knowing) and al-'Adl (the Most Just). He has put us in this specific situation for a reason. Before embracing Islam, many of those who later became beloved companions of the Prophet ﷺ used to hate Islam and did not come to it right away. It is our responsibility to keep striving towards better understanding of our din. If one struggles to recite the Qur'an properly, Allah ﷻ doubles the reward of this person simply because He sees the intention behind this act and rewards the struggle. So never give up hope. It's difficult to imagine that we would get more credit just for trying and struggling without any or not very much success in trying to get better at something else.

Often the Shaytan tries to derail us by suggesting things we would normally think of, such as: "Our reading is too slow;" "Why should we read the Qur'an when we don't understand it;" or "We're too old to learn." Shaytan fears the power of the Qur'an and he will do whatever is in his ability to pull us away from it. If we have good intentions, we will receive blessings by reciting or listening to the words of Allah ﷻ and will, as a result, get closer to Him.

When people are trying to learn a new language, they do not simply pick it up without effort. People study a language in many different ways, including listening to native speakers, regularly reading and practising speaking it, and getting tutored by a knowledgeable person. This process can at times be embarrassing, but most people will respect a person who makes an effort to learn something as difficult as a foreign language. It is important to bear in mind that while knowledge doesn't always come easily, the end result is always worth the effort, especially if that effort is toward learning the language of the Qur'an.

We all ask friends for a good book to read or check the list of the latest bestsellers. Why rely on the recommendations of people who have no bearing on our life? Take the recommendation of the best man on Earth, the Prophet Muhammad ﷺ, and pick up the greatest book of all time. It will elevate us to new heights, insha'Allah!

This would be a good time to mention a wonderful man that Sa'ad had the opportunity of meeting when he was visiting his in-laws. This man, an uncle at a small masjid in College Station, Texas, had retired a few years earlier. At the age of 70, he was quite fit, running a few miles each day when leaving the masjid after the *Fajr* (pre-dawn) prayer. This man realized that there had never been a *hafiz* (someone who has memorized the whole Qur'an by heart) in his family. Thus, he slowly began to memorize small portions after his retirement, and by the time Sa'ad had the honour of meeting him, he only had six *ajza* (portions) of the Qur'an left to memorize. Imagine, a man of such an age putting his mind to something and accomplishing it with such ease. This is the help that Allah ﷻ gives to any individual who makes an honest, sincere effort to grow closer to Him.

Finally, as educators, we know the importance of textbooks for any given class. These books have been designed to provide all of the knowledge necessary to learn the material as taught by the teacher in order to pass the class. In that same regard, our classroom is life itself, our teacher was the Messenger of Allah ﷺ, and our textbook is the Holy Qur'an. We will have to take our final exam on the Day of Judgment. We would call people who hoped to pass their final exams but discarded their textbooks hopeless. Simlarly, how do we think we can get through the trials and tests of this world and of the hereafter without studying this textbook? "The Qur'an will be a proof for you or against you." (Hadith) Everyday in our prayer we ask Allah ﷺ:

Guide us on the straight path. The path of those who have been favored by You. (Qur'an 1:6-7)

Allah ﷺ answers that du'a in the beginning of the very next surah:

This is the book in which there is no doubt, a guidance for all mankind. (Qur'an 2:2)

Allah ﷺ has answered our prayer for guidance in the Holy Qur'an: it is now time that we implement that answer in our lives.

PRACTICAL SOLUTIONS

- Read at least a small portion of the Qur'an everyday. Ideally, at least one page a day, but do whatever amount works for you and you can keep up regularly.
- Read an English translation of the Arabic original.
- After you recite, ask Allah ﷺ to accept your recitation and let what you recite, read and understand be reflected in your actions.
- Attend a class of commentary on the Qur'an that is taught by a scholar.
- Sit with a teacher and learn how to recite the Qur'an properly.
- Begin memorizing the short chapters of the Qur'an.

First Question on the Day of Judgment

Prayer

Salah was a gift from Allah ﷻ to His beloved ﷺ at the most trying period of the Prophet's life. The Quraysh had been boycotting the Muslims for over two years, a time in which the difficulty and starvation had reached such an extent that the people performing *tawaf* (circumambulation) of the Ka'bah miles away from this valley could hear the cries of the children. It was as a result of this boycott that the Prophet's dear wife and support of over twenty years, Khadijah ﷺ, and his uncle Abu Talib, who had been his protector and guardian since his early years, both died. Thereafter, the Prophet ﷺ went to Ta'if to spread the din and was chased out by the children and street urchins of the town who pelted him with rocks until his sandals became caked with blood.

At this time of great difficulty and stress, Allah ﷻ sent relief and glad tidings to the Prophet ﷺ in the form of an amazing journey known as *Isra'* (night journey) and *Mi'raj* (ascension). It was on this journey that the Messenger of Allah ﷺ travelled from Makkah to Jerusalem and then to the heavens where he met Allah ﷻ in a manner that only Allah ﷻ knows. Anytime people attend the court of a great king or ruler, the king will not let them leave except without giving them parting gifts to display his generosity and wealth. On the journey of Isra' and Mi'raj, the Prophet ﷺ met the King of all kings, and was given a few great gifts. One of these gifts was the salah. It is important to note that salah was particularly given to the Prophet ﷺ at this time of great difficulty, so we should think about what it can do for us in our daily lives and times of need. This meeting with Allah ﷻ re-energized the Messenger ﷺ in his mission, and it is in that light that we should look at the statement of the Prophet ﷺ when he said, "Salah is the Mi'raj of the believer." (Hadith)

He used the same word, Mi'raj, which described his ascension to the heavens to meet Allah ﷻ as a description of salah. Salah is the daily support in our busy schedules and times of difficulty that reminds us of the purpose of our lives.

Realize that salah will be the first question asked of us in the hereafter. We will not only be asked about whether or not we performed our salah, but also about the quality of our prayer. Therefore, we should really be conscious of what our answer will be. Most of us know the answer but do not want to think about it.

Shaytan works to divert us from our prayer and from thinking about the consequences of not praying as well. If we do manage to pray, Shaytan will not leave us alone. Rather, he will try to lead us away from having *khushu'* (focus) in our salah. He will try his hardest to distract us during our prayer, causing us to think about everything else except Allah ﷻ. All of us can attest to the fact that the strangest thoughts and worries plague our minds during prayer. This is the work of Shaytan. There is a famous story of a man who had hid his wealth in a particular spot for safekeeping but later forgot where he put it. As a result, this man came to Imam Abu Hanifah ؓ looking for help. The Imam suggested to this man that he pray two *rak'ah*s (cycles) of *nafl* (supererogatory or voluntary) prayer.

The man did as he was told and while he was praying, he remembered where he buried his wealth. He quickly left the prayer and unearthed his wealth. He was so happy that he ran to the imam and thanked him and inquired as to how he knew to give this solution. Imam Abu Hanifah ؓ simply answered that he thought that once the man had begun his prayer, this action would be so hated by Shaytan that the Devil would do anything to pull this man away from his prayer. As a result, Shaytan came and informed the man of the location of his wealth. The imam then asked the man whether or not he finished the prayer. The man replied by saying that he did not to which the imam responded that those two rak'ahs were more valuable than the entire Earth and what it contained.

Think about the last time any of us missed the Fajr prayer. Did we try to justify why we did not need to wake up? Perhaps we thought "I need some extra sleep to pass an important exam," "I stayed up too late," or "it's too cold." Certainly not many people would miss waking up early to take an exam, to get to work, or to catch a flight. This example should make us reflect upon whether or not we are giving salah the importance it deserves.

Additionally we need to be conscious of how we perform our salah. If we had the opportunity to meet someone famous like the Prime Minister or the President, we would make sure we were dressed appropriately, be on time, and try to spend as much time as possible with this person. Furthermore, how many of us would go to a job interview or go ask a potential father-in-law for his son's/daughter's hand in marriage in our pajamas? How many of us would come late? How many of us would let our breath smell? This is only an interview for a job or meeting a potential spouse, but during salah we are meeting our Creator and Benefactor and should think about each salah as an interview to secure our place in Jannah with our Lord. When we pray Fajr, for example, it should be unthinkable to stand before Allah ﷻ wearing the same nasty clothes we slept in during the night before while we speak His beautiful words with foul-smelling morning breath.

If we do wake up for Fajr, how many of us perform the quickest wudu' and then make sure to read the shortest surah possible? How many of us fail to remember or reflect upon what we recited from the Qur'an? The trick we really need to worry about is the excuses we give ourselves: "It's okay if I missed a prayer. Allah ﷻ is all Merciful and most Forgiving, so He will forgive me". Insha'Allah, it is the gift of Allah ﷻ to forgive us, but Allah ﷻ knows our intentions, and He knows that we had the time and capability to pray properly. We may be able to fool our teachers, bosses, and even our parents, but we cannot deceive Allah ﷻ.

Many young people have a dangerous practice of deceiving themselves about the necessity and importance of salah in their daily lives. They think that they will have time to pray in the future and plan to start praying regularly when they get old. But how can we guarantee that we will live that long? How can we start the practice of salah and do it consistently in our old age when we've spent a lifetime disparaging the importance of this sacred act? It is necessary to know that old habits die hard, and by neglecting the salah when we are young, we may never be able to return back to it. These are whispers from Shaytan,

The one who whispers into the hearts of mankind.
(Qur'an 114:5)

and they are aimed to lead us astray. Many of us can think of people whom we knew at a young age that passed away earlier than they thought they would. Many of these individuals had those exact thoughts in their minds, but their time ran out and they passed away without being able to make up their missed prayers.

We need to understand that prayer is a means of benefit to all of us. The Messenger of Allah ﷺ asked his companions what they would say about a person whose home was in front of a river and he had to leave his home five times a day, going across that river. The companions replied by saying that this person would be free of any dirt. The Prophet ﷺ told the companions that this was the effect of prayer. In another narration, a man came to the Prophet ﷺ seeking to be punished because he had committed an act with a woman that he should not have. The Prophet ﷺ instructed the man to sit with him. A short while thereafter the call for prayer was given and they stood up to pray. Upon completion of the prayer, the Prophet ﷺ stood to leave the masjid. The man ran after the Prophet ﷺ reminding him that he still needed to be punished. The Prophet ﷺ turned to the man and asked if he had not prayed. The man replied in the affirmative, to which the Prophet ﷺ explained to him that the prayer wipes away clean what was done between the two prayers.

Even the act of purifying oneself before beginning the prayer is blessed. Wudu', or ablution, requires that certain body parts be washed. When the body parts are cleansed, so is the soul of the individual. So when people do wudu', and wash their hands, the sins of their hands fall away, when the rinse their mouths out, the sins of their tongues fall away, and subsequently the sins fall away from all the corresponding body parts. Allah ﷻ has given us so many ways to be forgiven and enter Jannah.

PRACTICAL SOLUTIONS

- Make sure to do the best wudu' possible.
- Remember that you are standing in prayer in front of Allah ﷻ and be aware that He is watching you.
- Recite all parts of the prayer slowly and with concentration.
- Move from one position of the prayer to another in an unhurried way until you have completed all the revelant prayers.
- Perform the prayers that are part of the Sunnah.

Help! I Need Somebody!
Supplication

One of the most underappreciated, yet one of the greatest gifts Allah ﷻ has given us is the ability to supplicate to Him. In fact, when looking at all of the acts of worship, it is this specific act about which the Prophet ﷺ said, "Supplication is the essence of worship." (Hadith)

Our scholars regularly expound upon this Hadith, explaining the two main reasons why this act is the essence of worship. The first reason is that people who supplicate complete the requirement of calling upon Allah ﷻ, which is mentioned in the Qur'an. Secondly, these people also realize that it is only Allah ﷻ who can fulfill the needs of people. When an individual sincerely and wholeheartedly supplicates to Allah ﷻ, how can He not respond? According to the Hadith, Allah ﷻ always answers the du'a of an individual either in this life or the next and He may answer our du'as in ways that are not always apparent to us.

In fact, when we read in the Qur'an of the few times the companions of the Prophet ﷺ asked him a question, those situations were so dear to Allah ﷻ that He preserved them exactly as they were asked. We often refer to these verses as the *ya'salunaka* ("they ask you") verses. In these verses, Allah ﷻ starts by saying "they ask you concerning..." and He then orders the Prophet ﷺ to respond with, "say..." and the given reply. In these verses, the question and answer has been preserved by Allah ﷻ exactly as it was asked. And the manner in which it is preserved shows that Allah ﷻ is informing the Prophet ﷺ

that they are asking a particular question so reply to them with the given answer. Yet, one of the questions the Prophet 🕊 was asked was so beloved to Allah 🕊 that He answers it Himself without using this same format. He says,

And when my servant asks about Me, tell him that I am near. I answer the call of the caller when he calls upon Me, so respond to Me and believe in Me so that you may be righteous. (Qur'an 2:186)

Since this question was asking about Allah's response to the du'a of the believer, Allah 🕊 showed how quickly He will respond to the believer by actually responding to the question Himself in the Qur'an without the Prophet 🕊 as an intermediary.

At times, Shaytan will make us feel that our du'as have not been accepted and will cause us to have less faith in or to question Allah 🕊 – and this can result in us no longer wanting to supplicate. On the Day of Judgment, however, a person will see a large mountain of good deeds and will ask from where they had come. The person will be told these were all of their du'as that were not answered in the world but whose reward was reserved for the hereafter. Upon seeing the immense reward these unanswered du'as have earnt, this person will say to Allah 🕊 that he wished none of his du'as had been answered in the dunya.

Du'as are answered in different ways. The first way in which a du'a may be answered is that what we ask for is given immediately. The second way is that what we ask for may be given later. The third way in which a du'a may be answered is that Allah 🕊 will give us something better in its place. If it has not been answered in any of these ways, then Allah 🕊 will remove a hardship from us. Finally, if not answered in any of the previous ways, Allah 🕊 will grant a reward in place of that du'a, that will be given to the believer on the Day of Judgment and this is the best way to have our du'as answered. It is important, therefore, to remember that our du'as are heard by Allah 🕊 and we should not be hasty in wanting a response. Many of us have come very close in our lives to getting in severe car accidents, and what may have saved us was a du'a that we made when we were younger but was apparently left unanswered, where in reality the response was reserved to save us from that particular calamity.

There are secrets to du'a that, if channelled, will cause a believer to benefit fully from the potential of his or her du'as. We live in a world where our actions will yield different responses and results depending upon various situations. For example, if any given person speaks jokingly about committing a terror-related crime in the privacy of their home, that comment would most likely soon be forgotten and no harm would come of it. However, if this same comment is made in a different setting, perhaps at an airport, the repercussions could be very serious. This person might come under suspicion and suffer adverse consequences. The same concept can be applied to our acts of worship. If situated in a certain time or place, an act of worship may yield more reward than usual. Du'a, not only being an act of worship, but as the hadith states, the core of worship, is no different. Time is one great factor that unlocks the potential of du'a and opens up the window of acceptance.

Du'as made in certain times and situations are more likely to be accepted. It comes in various Ahadith that, among other times, du'a is accepted between the time of the adhan and iqamah, between the two khutbahs at Jumu'ah prayer, in one particular hour on the day of Friday, during travel, during sickness, and at the end of fasting. SubhanAllah, many of us are constantly in these situations on a weekly, if not daily, basis. If we take a few moments to supplicate to Allah ﷻ, then the effects of our supplication will likely be felt and seen in unimaginable ways. It also comes in Hadith that a du'a made after each prescribed prayer is accepted. This principle is applicable to any act of worship: when one has completed fasting or given charity then they should supplicate to Allah ﷻ.

The Qur'an highlights this point beautifully in Surah al-Baqarah. Allah ﷻ relates the story of the prophets Ibrahim and

Ismail ﷺ when they were ordered to build the Ka'bah. Upon being given this task, father and son set out to reestablish the House of Allah. They fulfilled this arduous assignment with true elation and submission – upon its completion, the Qur'an relates the actions of father and son:

And when Ibrahim raised the foundations of the house with Ismail, [they said] "Our Lord, accept this from us, [for] indeed You are the All-Hearing, All-Knowing." (Qur'an 2:127)

SubhanAllah, what an amazing lesson lies within these few words. Here are two prophets of Allah ﷺ, having undertaken the task of rebuilding the Ka'bah, and thereafter, having done so, their first act is to supplicate to Allah ﷺ asking Him to accept their endeavor. How many times have we supplicated to Allah ﷺ asking Him merely to accept our compulsory acts of worship? We take our worship for granted, assuming that Allah ﷺ will accept it, but there is no guarantee. If two prophets are concerned about their acts of worship being accepted, especially an act that they were ordered to do directly by Allah ﷺ, then it behooves us to show that same concern with any act of worship that we perform.

Aside from making du'a at certain times, there are certain conditions that we should seek to fulfill. In a famous Hadith of the Prophet ﷺ, we learn about a man who was on a journey and was completely overtaken by the difficulty of his situation. While he is dusty and dishevelled, he raises his hands and cries out to his Lord for help. But the Hadith ends by the Prophet ﷺ asking how the du'a of a man like this can be accepted when his food and nourishment was *haram* (prohibited), his drink was haram, and his clothes were haram. In this Hadith, we find that one of the keys to attaining the acceptance of Allah ﷺ is by keeping our lives filled with as many halal things as possible. This makes sense even just by thinking about it for a moment.

Imagine if a person tells us not to do something and we still do it. And then we go to the person and ask for something. Why should that person give us what we have asked for, especially when we did something that person did not want us to do? In that same light, why should Allah ﷻ give us what we want and ask for, when we do not do the things that He has asked us to do and when we do not stay away from the things He has asked us to stay away from?

It is also important for us to learn the proper manner of making du'a. Although there is no required way of making du'a, there are recommended ways to do so. What we should always keep in mind is that anytime we perform an act of worship, whether it requires wudu' or not, we should make a conscious effort to stay in wudu'. In fact, the scholars recommend that people be in wudu' at all times. It is especially true that when we want to make du'a, we should make sure we are in a state of wudu'. Thereafter, we should compare du'a with a sandwich. Imagine the pieces of bread as being the praises of Allah ﷻ. We should begin and end our du'a by praising our Creator. Then we should think of all the extras – the vegetables, the condiments, etc. – as sending peace and blessings on the Prophet ﷺ. Some scholars have gone as far as to say that a du'a that is sandwiched by the sending of peace and blessings on the Prophet ﷺ will never be rejected because Allah ﷻ would never reject anything that is surrounded by mention of His beloved. Finally, the crux of your du'a should be the meat of the sandwich. This should be what you are seeking or asking from Allah ﷻ. The order would, a result, be (1) praising Allah ﷻ, (2) sending peace and blessings upon the Prophet ﷺ, (3) asking what you are seeking, (4) sending peace and blessings on the Prophet ﷺ, and (5) praising Allah ﷻ.

Furthermore, when supplicating, we should yearn and be very sincere in our du'a. Imagine if a poor man comes to us on the street asking for money. But, rather than asking, he demands it as if it is in his right, or in a very haughty and proud manner. We would be appalled by his approach and might not give him anything. In that same light, when we supplicate to Allah ﷻ, we shouldn't just ask Him in a manner that it doesn't seem important to us. In that case why should Allah ﷻ answer our du'a? When we make du'a we should put our heart into it, yearn, beg, plead, shed tears, and ask Allah ﷻ as true slaves should ask of their Lord. Another way to look at it is, when we were younger, we wanted some toy or plaything from our parents. We would beg and beg our parents until we got that toy we desired. That is how we should ask Allah ﷻ, and it is du'a such as this that are dear to Him.

Finally, we want to mention the power of du'a by giving a personal example. Almost four years ago, Sa'ad was involved in a major accident when he fell approximately 25 feet while climbing a tree. The damage that he suffered was so severe that many of the nurses and doctors who examined him said that he would not survive. In fact, he was given a generous 5% chance of survival. His liver had grade four or five lacerations, his hepatic artery was severed, and he had severe internal bleeding, amongst other problems. A few days after his accident his lungs had collapsed. Things looked very bleak for Sa'ad, but Muslims in various communities prayed to Allah ﷻ. When there was no other option left, the doctors decided to operate on him as a last resort, as the surgery was extremely risky. Yet, when they went in to fix him up they found that things suddenly were not as bad as they had seemed. All the signs had pointed towards the need for difficult and dangerous surgery, but the prayers made by so many people had had an effect and what had looked like possible death for Sa'ad suddenlty turned into him walking out of the hospital nineteen days later. This is the power of du'a. If we feel that it is too late for us to improve, remember that the power of du'a helped to save a person who was almost dead, so the power of prayer can save a soul that we feel may almost be spiritually dead.

I (Sa'ad) want to thank the Jondy family, the Shah family, the Iqbal family, and all the other families and individuals that assisted my family in that time of difficulty and supplicated for me. I can never repay you, and I may not know who you are, but I pray that Allah ﷻ rewards you with an infinite reward.

PRACTICAL SOLUTIONS

- Supplicate consistently.
- Supplicate for your iman, knowledge, family, health, wealth, etc.
- Supplicate for others (when you do this, the angels supplicate for you).
- Remember the blessed names of Allah ﷻ when starting your du'as. For example, "Ya Gafoor (The Forgiver), forgive me for the sins I did knowingly and unknowingly."
- Send *salawat* (peace and blessings) on the Prophet ﷺ in you du'a.
- Before you go to sleep, ask Allah ﷻ to make your coming days better than the previous ones spiritually, mentally, physically, intellectually, etc.

I've Been Thinkin' About You
Dhikr

Imagine standing on the front lines anticipating the beginning of a battle. How much would fear have penetrated our hearts? What would we be thinking? What would we be doing? Chances are, we might be thinking about our loved ones, or we might just be very scared. What would be our state of mind when we finally met our enemy? Imagine looking into the eyes of someone who really wanted to kill us. In such an intense moment, where it seems that nothing can be going through a person's mind or heart except the task at hand, Allah 🕮 commands the believers to act as follows:

> *Oh you who believe, when you meet an opposing enemy, be firm and remember Allah excessively so that you may be successful.* (Qur'an 8:45)

SubhanAllah, in this intense moment of possible confusion and chaos, Allah 🕮 orders believers to do dhikr. We may be asking ourselves why, but the reason is simple:

> *Without doubt, by the remembrance of Allah do the hearts become tranquil.* (Qur'an 13:28)

Simply put, dhikr is remembrance. In the context of this verse and the daily life of a believer, dhikr is the remembrance of Allah 🕮. Growing up, we may have learned various *adhkar* (plural of dhikr) that we use regularly. In times of happiness, grief, or in any matter, we say *alhamdulillah* (all praise is for

Allah). In fact, this is one of the signs of a believer according to the Prophet ﷺ who said, "How strange is the affair of the believer, everything is good. If a test were to befall him he says 'alhamdulillah' and if something good were to befall him he says 'alhamdulillah'." (Hadith)

In times of attributing an act or a situation to Allah ﷻ, we say *masha'Allah*. In times of exalting Allah's ﷻ greatness, we say *Allahu Akbar* (Allah is the greatest). Every situation in our lives has a prayer attached to it, that allows us to remember Allah ﷻ. Applying this practice of dhikr is vitally important because everything in our lives constantly takes us away from the remembrance of Allah ﷻ. Our hectic schedules divert our attention from the remembrance of Allah ﷻ, which should make us feel truly empty. But by simply implementing the small adhkar highlighted in Qur'an and Hadith we can easily incorporate the remembrance of Allah ﷻ back into our lives and lift ourselves spiritually.

Without doubt, there has never been anyone busier in this world than the Prophet ﷺ. It was his responsibility to spread the revelation of the Qur'an and deliver the message of Islam to the entire world. Or, to put it bluntly, it was his responsibility to spread a message of salvation that would guide those heading along the path to hell towards the way to heaven. We are constantly complaining that we are always busy: we have to study for a test, go to work, take care of our families, or many other things. Yet, the Prophet ﷺ had the awesome task of bringing the final message to humanity. If sheer workload was a genuine excuse, it would be understandable if he was unable to remember Allah ﷻ regularly. Yet, his life was the embodiment of the remembrance of Allah ﷻ. In fact, it comes in hadith that the Prophet ﷺ was sleeping when two angels visited him. One angel went to wake him from his sleep when the second angel stopped him. When the first angel inquired as to why the second angel had stopped him, the second angel told him it was because the Prophet ﷺ was sleeping. At that point the first angel replied by saying that, "His eyes may sleep, but his heart is awake in the remembrance of Allah." (Hadith)

The Prophet ﷺ further confirmed this statement during another incident in which 'A'ishah ﵂ asked the Prophet ﷺ about his sleep to which he said, "My eyes may sleep, but my heart is awake with the remembrance of Allah." (Hadith) SubhanAllah, the Prophet's heart was so immersed in the remembrance of Allah ﷻ that it would continue even while he slept.

So why be regular in the remembrance of Allah ﷻ? Our remembrance keeps us grounded in our faith. Just as humanity has certain inherent checks and balances that exist to help us stay in line, regular dhikr is a way to keep us focused on the right path. For example, our government has different branches that make sure power is equally distributed, and in our workplaces and schools we have different levels of hierarchy to maintain a proper hierarchy. This is also present in our daily interactions with the people in our lives. Our behaviour reflects our morality and faith; therefore, we are more conscious of how we act and what we say around people whose respect we hope to gain. This could be our parents, grandparents, certain friends, teachers or employers. During the time of the companions, the Sahabah were extremely ashamed to commit an action that was even remotely disliked by the Prophet ﷺ. Although the Prophet ﷺ is not here today, we live in the presence of his faithful inheritors, namely the scholars, and we should have the same mindset.

Continuing with this principle, humanity should naturally be embarrassed to do anything wrong in front of Allah ﷻ. The problem is that people forget Allah ﷻ because they cannot see Him with their own eyes. But one way in which we can constantly remind ourselves of His existence is by remembering Him. By constantly having His name on our tongue and in our hearts, we will naturally be drawn to Him, recognizing that He has power over all things, and that He has created us, provides for us, guides us, rewards us, forgives us, and punishes us when we do not turn to Him. If we always remember Him and recall that He is the One who rewards or punishes, we will change the way we act and keep away from sinning.

PRACTICAL SOLUTIONS

- Memorize the du'as connected with everyday acts (i.e., du'a for waking up in the morning, du'a for eating etc.) as they are means to remember Allah ﷻ as we go through our daily lives, as taught to us by the Prophet ﷺ.
- Carry a *tasbih* (dhikr beads) in your pocket. This will remind you to do dhikr any time you put your hands in your pockets.

Lean on Me

Good Company

When it comes to judging who we are, there is almost no better way to describe ourselves than by the company we keep. The Prophet ﷺ mentioned that people will be with the ones whom they love in the hereafter. For many of us in high school and college, the people whom we are with the majority of the time are our friends. We talk to them, hang out with them, have deep discussions with them, ask them for advice, along with many other things.

Even our Prophet ﷺ almost never went anywhere without a few companions. Here was a man who was protected by Allah ﷻ, but he still kept good company constantly. Even before the first revelation, his best friend was Abu Bakr ﷺ. During his prophethood, we find that on the two greatest journeys that he took, he chose the two greatest companions to accompany him. When he made the migration (*hijrah*) from Makkah to Madinah, he was accompanied by the greatest of the companions, Abu Bakr ﷺ. And when he journeyed from Makkah to Jerusalem and then to the heavens, he was accompanied by the greatest of the angels, Jibreel ﷺ.

It is so important when we are bombarded with temptations to have friends who can help us get through tough times, help us remember our ultimate purpose in this world, and remind us that this world is temporary and that we are travelers headed for a greater destination.

We hang out the most with our friends during our teenage years, sometimes more than with our parents, families, or teachers. For many of us, one of the motivations to go to school is to see our friends. So knowing that friends play an intricate part in our daily lives, why not invest in friends who can help us be the best in this world and in the hereafter? One way we can do this is to attend a religious study circle.

We have gatherings for many purposes. We get together with our classmates before an exam, or we get together to play video games or a sport, but we often do not get together to take some time to remember Allah ﷻ – for example, helping each other memorize Qur'an. Embarrassment is minimized when we learn the Qur'an together at an older age than is the common practice. An easy way to find supportive friends is to start a study circle. When we were young we had such a study circle (*halaqa*). Once every week we got together and looked at the basics of Islam, the life of the Prophet ﷺ, the Qur'an, memorized portions of the Qur'an, and discussed contemporary topics. We did it for at least six years and we can both attest that it truly was a blessing. It made us become consistent in picking up the Qur'an and learning Hadith in order to help us change our lives.

This circle won't turn anyone into a scholar, but it will instill a love of learning about the din, and help us to stay focused on the purpose of our creation. Having friends join us in doing this will help everyone stay consistent and provide the support in school and college that we all need. An added benefit is that if we start this off ourselves then we will also share the reward of every individual who participates in learning.

Another way of encouraging positive peer pressure is through youth groups. A youth group can be in a local masjid, high school, community centre, or even at our homes. These organizations already might have a program for "play and pray" in an Islamic environment. Many times teenagers tell us, "I went but it was not for me," or that "they are not cool," or "too conservative," or "too liberal". But be honest, are we really giving that group an honest chance? When Habeeb was younger, his dad wanted him to go to a Central Zone MYNA (Muslim Youth of North America) Camp, and he was not really excited about it. He even said to himself that he will make sure to give his father good reasons why this would be a waste of money after he got back. After all, it was held in the winter and Habeeb didn't want to miss basketball practice for anything. But, alhamdullilah, his dad had one of the older youths of the community call to convince him. It made him attend the camp with an open mind and he will tell anyone that it was one of the best things that happened to him. He was able to meet some cool Muslim students who played sport, did well in school, and still practiced the din. The speakers there made him and the youth like him proud of who they were, while increasing their knowledge of the religion and encouraging them to grow closer to Allah 徽.

Many of the older youth who've attended camps and conferences like this can attest that attending such a program was life changing. Unfortunately, many of us feel that these programs are not worth our time. It is extremely important for us to keep an open mind and see what sorts of people we hang around with. A good tool to gauge the company to keep is by asking ourselves questions such as, "Do they help me to remember Allah 徽?"; "Do they remind me of the Prophet 徽 and his companions?"; "Do I remember Jannah and Jahannam when I am around these people?"; and "Do these brothers or sisters encourage me to go to the masjid or to pray and read Qur'an?" Those who obey Allah 徽 and His Messenger 徽 are described as:

> *Those are the people who Allah blessed with them [companions] from the prophets, the truthful ones, the martyrs, and the righteous ones, and what a great company that is.* (Qur'an 4:69)

And the Prophet 徽 has even reminded us that "A person is with whom he loves." (Hadith)

We should also make it a point to find the scholars and righteous people in our community and keep their company. The Prophet 徽 said, "The scholars are the inheritors of the prophets." (Hadith) Many of us have an immediate aversion to the word "scholar". We immediately think of people with long beards dressed in traditional clothing who are quick to judge us. The reality is that these people have been trained to help others and will often be the last to be judgemental. Especially in today's age when we have an increasing number of young scholars who have grown up in America, Britain and other Western countries, we can benefit from those who know "where we're coming from" and who have inherited the wealth of the prophets. They have had many of the same experiences that we have had and been able to acquire knowledge and a closeness to Allah 🕮 that we should seek to acquire too. The prophets are the most beloved creation of Allah 🕮, and He has given a special wealth to His beloved servants. When they leave this world they leave behind that inheritance to specific people, the scholars of today.

The importance of friendship is mentioned in the Qur'an where Allah 🕮 says,

> **Woe to me, if only I did not take him as a friend.**
> (Qur'an 25:28)

This verse has an interesting story from the time of the Prophet 🕮. It was the tradition of the Arabs to throw a feast when they returned safely from a journey, as journeys then were dangerous and risky. Thus, when 'Utbah ibn Mu'it returned from a journey he had a feast for the noblemen of Makkah, and among those he invited was the Messenger of Allah 🕮. When the food was brought out, the Prophet 🕮 refused to eat unless 'Utbah, one of the foremost enemies of Islam, said the *shahadah* (the testimony of faith by which a non-believer becomes a Muslim). The Arabs were then, and are still today, known for their hospitality. If someone was not fed by a host, it was looked down upon. So when the Prophet 🕮 refused to eat, 'Utbah did whatever was necessary to make him eat. Thus he said the shahadah and the Prophet 🕮 became happy and ate. The following day Abu Jahl heard of what had transpired. When he saw 'Utbah he refused to speak to or interact with him claiming that 'Utbah had now betrayed them and become a Muslim. 'Utbah explained that he had only said what he did to save face from the potential humiliation that would follow if the Arabs found out he had not done what was necessary to feed his guests. Abu Jahl told him to prove himself by going to the Prophet ﷺ to denounce Islam in front of everyone and spit in his face. 'Utbah, to please his friend, did this very act.

On the Day of Judgment, those who enter hell are gathered in the hellfire; various disbelievers will see some of the believers there and exclaim that at least they, the disbelievers, were able to enjoy their lives in the previous world. The believers had not only wasted their lives in the previous world but were now suffering the same torment as the disbelievers. Allah ﷻ will hate this statement so much that He will order that any person with even a mustard seed's worth of faith in his heart – anyone who has said the shahadah – be removed from hell. At this point 'Utbah will cry out,

Woe to me, if only I did not take him as a friend.
(Qur'an 25:28)

'Utbah had taken back his shahadah in the dunya for the sake of pleasing his friend, Abu Jahl, and as a result was no longer included with those who have testified at least once to the Oneness of Allah ﷻ. What a horrible situation to be in!

Everything comes down to this question, "Are we preparing for the hereafter by remaining on the path we are on with our current friends?" This is not to say we should give up on any of our friends, looking to leave them behind if we want to lead a life of piety. Rather, we should think that if we really care for our friends, then we would make an even greater effort to surround ourselves with the kind of good company we would hope would attract them as well. And, if they aren't attracted to that kind of good company, then at least they can benefit from the good we've learned. The reality is that if we do not surround ourselves with good company, Shaytan will easily pick us off. A hungry wolf attacks the sheep that strays from the herd; Shaytan preys on the believer that stays alone.

PRACTICAL SOLUTIONS

- See if the local masjid has a youth group.
- If not, make enquiries with a national Muslim youth organization to see if they have anything established in your area.
- Check out Muslim student societies at your local high school or university to see if they can set up a youth program.
- Start your own halaqa – ask a local scholar or an experienced youth activist to help guide you in this process. If you start one you'll share in the reward of all those who take part.

There's No Place Like Home

Masjid

Anyone who has lived away from home for any period of time will say that there is no place like home. Although while we are young and living at home we cannot wait to leave, the moment that we are away from home and out of our comfort zone, part of us yearns to go back. The same idea is true for the believer.

As Muslims, the house of Allah 🕮 – the *masjid* (mosque) – is our spiritual home, and where we can go to renew our faith. According to the Messenger of Allah 🕮, "The most beloved places to Allah are the masajid (mosques)." (Hadith) The masajid were established as places for believers to gather together to remember their Lord. When we at look the life of the Prophet 🕮, he always lived where there was a masjid. For the 13 years he preached in Makkah, the Prophet 🕮 lived near the Ka'bah in Masjid al-Haram. When the Prophet 🕮 was forced to migrate from Makkah to Madinah, he established a masjid when he stopped at Quba, and he again established a masjid upon arriving at Madinah. It was always a very high priority for the Prophet 🕮 to make sure that there was a place for prayer and a meeting place for the believers.

The importance of a masjid to a community is evident today. Communities that have a central place where believers can gather together to learn, meet, and pray are better established than communities without a mosque, even if the latter has a larger Muslim population. The masjid plays that role of a gas station for the believer. When the fuel tank of iman runs low, a believer can quickly go to the masjid and spend some time there, replenishing the tank before going out and giving to the community.

There is no doubting that school and college have become a spiritual battleground. On a regular basis our iman is attacked from all angles by Shaytan and our nafs. The benefit of having a masjid is that it provides us with a safe haven where many temptations are no longer around us. Furthermore, the prayers that are offered in congregation in the masjid are twenty-seven times greater in reward than those offered individually. As we are all in need of every good deed possible, praying five prayers in congregation in the masjid can earn us 135 rewards!

Also, in school and college, we find that our schedules are extremely busy. Many of us want to improve ourselves by fasting, praying five times a day, and other acts that would bring us closer to Allah ﷻ. One act of devotion that many of us hope we might become consistent in is performing the tahajjud prayer. This prayer is one that brings servants extremely close to Allah ﷻ as He calls out to humanity in the last third of each night, seeing who is awake and asking of Him so He may grant what they seek. He also calls out to those seeking forgiveness so that He may forgive them. Those rare people who stand up in prayer at night are very fortunate. But with school schedules being so hectic, it is difficult to always get up and pray. This is where the masjid comes in. There is a Hadith related by 'Uthman ﷺ whereby he narrates the Prophet ﷺ as saying, "Whosoever prays 'Isha in congregation will receive half of the night as reward. And whosoever the pre-dawn prayer (Fajr) in congregation will receive (the other) half of the night as reward." (Hadith) This secret is integral in advancing in the din. Imagine, going to 'Isha (the evening prayer) and Fajr prayer in the masjid. Even if we spend the entire night (between 'Isha and Fajr) studying for school, we still receive the reward of spending the entire night in prayer!

Many masajid now cater more for Muslim youth, although much more could still be done. The newer masajid have built some sports and social facilities that allow the youth to spend their free time in good company. People often ask us where they can find good company. The answer is simple. If a person is looking to meet righteous people who are close to Allah ﷻ, what better place to find them than in His house?

Our environment always works to shape how we think and act. So just being in the house of Allah ﷻ, even sitting in it to study when we were students, is still beneficial. Sitting in the masjid allows us to share in the blessings that are showered upon the house of Allah ﷻ, and, with this habit, we will have the opportunity to observe all the congregational prayers there. On those days when we don't have work to do, we will still be in the masjid out of habit, and we can then pick up the Qur'an or a book on Hadith or some other religious book.

In the end, we know that we would never invite an enemy into our homes. Most people will only invite those whom they love into their homes. If Allah ﷻ invites us into His home, then we should accept His invitation in hopes that He will invite us again and again and that we can spend time with the Host. Most importantly, if Allah ﷻ continues to invite us to His home in this world and we make all efforts to accept His invitation, we can hope that He too will invite us to share from His never-ending bounties in the hereafter.

PRACTICAL SOLUTIONS

- If you have the ability to, try to live near a masjid.
- Make spending time at your local masjid part of your schedule.
- Volunteer to help out at your local masjid.
- Try starting out by praying 'Isha and Fajr at the masjid.

26

Never Give Up
Hope

Giving up can be easy, and sometimes it can seem like the only way out. After years of striving to grow closer to Allah ﷻ and please Him but still falling into sin, after years of trying to wake up for Fajr but still sleeping through, after a lifetime of trying to lower our eyes but still not being able to control our gaze, who can blame us for wanting to give up? After all, we've already sinned so much that there really isn't any turning back. Sound familiar? Of course it does. This is what Shaytan whispers to us on a daily basis.

We are servants of Allah ﷻ. Any way we try to label ourselves, the fact is that our responsibility is to serve Him and our goal is to please Him.

> *And We have not created Jinn and mankind except to worship Me.* (Qur'an 51:56)

With all the challenges and tests we undergo in life, sometimes it is easy to be distracted from our goal.

> *Made beautified for mankind is their love for their desires from women, and children, and their wealth from their gold and their silver.* (Qur'an 3:14)

When we eventually see that we have been distracted and subsequently have strayed away from our goal, we promise ourselves that we will start anew and never return to sinful ways. Yet it seems that we always fall back to sinning.

Anytime we take two steps forward we end up going ten steps backwards. What is funny is that we aren't alone in feeling this way.

After having attended a gathering of the Prophet ﷺ, his companion Handhala ؓ returned to his family. His awareness and rememberance of Allah ﷻ then weakened compared to what it was when he was with the Prophet ﷺ. When he detected this, he immediately left home and began proclaiming that he was a hypocrite. When Abu Bakr ؓ heard what he was saying, he pulled him to one side and asked why he was saying such a thing. After all, it was impossible that such a great companion like Handhala ؓ could have become a hypocrite. Handhala ؓ began to describe his state to Abu Bakr ؓ, who admitted to feeling the same. They both rushed immediately to the Prophet ﷺ, explaining their discovery. The Prophet ﷺ calmed them down and assured them that had they been able to maintain the level of iman outside of his gatherings that they had when they were with him, then the angels would descend to the Earth and shake their hands.

The reality is that we may not always be able to maintain the level of iman we experience after listening to a lecture or during the month of Ramadan, and sometimes we fall deeply into sin after experiencing a brief religious awakening, but we should never get down on ourselves. In fact, look at the life of one of the greatest companions ever to live, 'Umar ibn Khattab ؓ, about whom the Prophet ﷺ said, "If there was a prophet to come after me, it would be 'Umar." (Hadith) Before embracing Islam, 'Umar ؓ had been a great enemy of the Muslims in Makkah. He awoke one day and left his home with the intention of murdering the Prophet ﷺ. Yet Allah ﷻ had greater plans for him, and the man, who in the morning sought to kill the Prophet ﷺ, had become a Muslim by the end of the day, and was now beseeching the Prophet ﷺ to permit the Muslims to proclaim Islam openly to the people of Makkah. When we look at our lives we see that many of us have done some horrible things, but none of us have ever contemplated, wished or thought of removing the Prophet ﷺ

from the Earth. The point is that we should never despair of the mercy of Allah ﷻ.

It comes in Hadith that there was a man who had killed ninety-nine men. He realized the error of his evil ways and wanted to rectify himself. He went to a righteous worshipper, explained his situation and asked if there was any hope left for him. The worshipper told him that the killer was doomed for his transgressions. This upset the killer very much and he killed the righteous worshipper to take his bloodly tally to a hundred people. Later he reflected upon his evil deeds again and decided that he wanted to change. He searched for and found a righteous scholar in his community. He went to the scholar and explained his situation fully. (We should note here the importance of seeking advice of righteous people who are knowledgeable. While there are many benefits to having the company of righteous people, we should seek advice from righteous people of knowledge who can help and guide us towards Allah ﷻ. The companions of the Prophet ﷺ were blessed enough to do so with the Messenger of Allah ﷺ, and we are fortunate in that we have his inheritors, the righteous scholars of religious learning.)

In any case to return to the story again, once the man explained his situation to the scholar, the scholar replied that there was still hope for him. He would have to repent for his sins and specifically move away from this city as the environment there would not help him to change and grow spiritually. The man set out to migrate to another city. On his way to this new city, he passed away. An angel of heaven and an angel of hell descended upon his body and both were confused when they saw the other, as each had come to claim the body. They both returned to Allah ﷻ to settle the matter. Allah ﷻ decreed that if the body was closer to his city of departure, then the angel of hell should claim the body, and if the body was closer to his destination, then the angel of heaven should claim the body. The body was in fact closer to the point of departure, but before the angels could return, Allah ﷻ caused the earth to constrict, making the man seem closer to his destination. Thus Allah ﷻ forgave a man who killed one hundred people because He saw the sincerity in his repentance. Truly Allah is Most Forgiving.

SubhanAllah, there are many stories that show the mercy of Allah ﷻ and His willingness to forgive. Many of us have heard the story of the prostitute who was forgiven and granted Jannah just because she brought water in her shoe from a well to give to a dog that was dying of thirst. Allah ﷻ is very quick to forgive and bring us back to Him. Look at Abu Sufyan ؓ who fought against the Prophet ﷺ for so many years. Allah ﷻ accepted him and he became a great Sahabi. Even his wife, Hind ؓ, the woman who was responsible for hiring Wahshi to murder the Prophet's beloved uncle, Hamza ؓ, and who ate of Hamza's liver, a contemptuous and barbaric act, was forgiven when she repented and accepted as a Muslim. Even the assassin Wahshi ؓ was forgiven too.

The point is that Allah ﷻ is quick to turn to us if we turn to Him,

Oh you who believe, turn to Allah in a sincere repentance.
(Qur'an 66:8)

and we must have the best opinion of our Lord, for as is stated in tradition, "I am as My servant thinks I am. If he remembers Me to himself, I remember him to Myself. If he makes mention of Me to a group, I make mention of him to a group greater than his. If he draws near to Me a hand's length, I draw near to him an arm's length. If he draws near to Me an arm's length, I draw near to him a fathom's length. If he comes to Me walking, I go to him running." (Hadith Qudsi)

Allah ﷻ Himself is telling the believers that He will come even quicker to us the moment we turn to Him. It is up to us to turn to Him. We should always be of the opinion that Allah ﷻ will forgive us and that we can turn back to Him at any time. This shouldn't become an excuse for us to sin, but in case we do trip and fall, we should not be embarrassed of repenting as Shaytan wants us to be. He whispers to us not to repent, claiming that we can never uphold our promise of abstaining from sin. It is

Shaytan who tells us not to repent because we should be too embarrassed to turn back to Allah ﷻ yet again. But Shaytan was the one who despaired and became rejected because of his leaving Allah ﷻ. We are amongst those who know that Allah ﷻ will forgive ours sins even if they pile up and reach the sky. And if we turn back again with sins piling up from the Earth to the heavens in sincere repentence, then Allah ﷻ has promised to forgive us. In fact, Allah ﷻ provides the greatest hope one can want when He says,

Say: Oh My servants who have transgressed against themselves, do not despair in the mercy of Allah. He will forgive you completely, and He is the Most-Forgiving, Most-Merciful. (Qur'an 39:53)

Sometimes after spending time with children, parents become annoyed and will say to their spouse, "Do you know what your child did today?" Many of us are guilty of it. The reality is that a child may have done something that was bad enough for a mother to attribute the child to its father or vice versa. Yet here in this verse, Allah ﷻ calls upon His servants as "My servants," and not just any of His servants, but those who transgressed and wronged themselves! Despite us doing wrong, Allah ﷻ is still claiming us as His own and telling us not to despair: if we turn back to Him in repentance, He will forgive our sins!

We can never and should never lose hope. Life is going to be difficult, but life itself is a struggle. The Prophet ﷺ said, "The world is a prison for the believer and a heaven for the disbeliever." (Hadith) We are locked up in our cells and looking out at the rest of the free world. But this is not the real, eternal life for the believers. We are imprisoned in it and will face the difficulties that one faces while in prison. But the reality is that we will be let out of our prisons to enter into a permanent blissful abode, which is heaven. We can never give up on the reality of that fact. There will be times when nothing we have written about here will be applicable to us, and there will be times when everything will be applicable to us. No matter what state we are in, we have to keep trying until we turn back towards our Lord. And on that beautiful day, when the deeds are laid out and everyone is judged, we will, insha'Allah, hear Allah ﷻ call onto us saying,

Oh you successful soul. Return to your Lord pleased and pleased-with! So enter into My submission, enter into my paradise! (Qur'an 89:27-30)

27

Small Deeds That Are Overlooked

Small and Consistent Actions

Pennies can, at times, be very annoying. As we're fishing through our pockets and searching for change at a vending machine, or looking through our coin holders at a toll, pennies get in the way. We would rather that those pennies weren't there and we could get rid of them somehow. Yet those same pennies that we feel are annoying can become deeds that enter us into Jannah.

Jannah isn't cheap, but every deed that we do will be taken into account.

> *So whosoever does a good deed equal to the weight of an atom will see* (their reward). *And whosoever does a bad deed equal to the weight of an atom will see* (their punishment). (Qur'an 99:7-8)

Sometimes the idea of a good deed is overwhelming. We think that we have to do amazing acts of worship and stand for long periods of the night while fasting all day to gain Allah's pleasure. However, the Prophet ﷺ made it clear the types of actions that Allah ﷻ loves, "The most beloved actions to Allah are those that are consistent, even if they are small." (Hadith) The deed itself does not have to be large to gain Allah's love. It is much better for us to give a small amount in charity regularly – for example, one dollar a week – than give a large amount at one time and not donate after that. The reason is simple. Allah ﷻ has given us life for a limited time on this Earth. Yet, even though we have only a limited time to do good deeds, we can attain a permanent abode in paradise. Similarly, a person who sins only for a limited time on this Earth can suffer a permanent punishment in hell. Why do we have such a short time on this Earth to prove ourselves? It is because Allah ﷻ knows that even if we were given one hundred years to live, or even an eternity, those years would be filled with good deeds, or, may Allah ﷻ protect us, with sins. As a result, if a person habitually gives in charity what he or she can afford every week, Allah ﷻ knows that if that person was to live forever, that small amount would be given in donation every week for eternity. And a person who gave a large donation once has not shown Allah ﷻ whether or not that was a one-time donation or whether it would be a constant good deed.

Deeds come in different forms. The Prophet ﷺ has specified in various hadith that normal everyday actions can be *sadaqah* (charity), actions that we would consider to be mundane such as smiling can be a means of reward. The Prophet ﷺ taught that, "Every Muslim has to give sadaqah." The people asked: "O Prophet of Allah, what about the one who has nothing?" He said: "He should work with his hands to give sadaqah." They asked: "If he cannot find [work]?" He replied: "He should help the needy who ask for help." They asked: "If he cannot do that?" He replied: "He should then do good deeds and shun evil, for this will be taken as sadaqah." (Hadith) In another narration, the Prophet ﷺ has stated that "Sadaqah is prescribed for every person every day the sun rises. To administer justice between two people is sadaqah. To assist a man upon his mount so that he may ride it is sadaqah. To place his luggage on the animal is sadaqah. To remove harm from the road is sadaqah. A good word is sadaqah. Each step taken toward prayer is sadaqah." (Hadith)

In yet another narration, the Prophet ﷺ made it clear that even a smile is considered to be a form of charity. These narrations all show that, against our common mistake not to consider regular acts as good deeds, our Prophet ﷺ advised the believers to protect themselves from the fire even through the donation of a date stone. Now, we might think "what can a date stone do?" But, we need to understand that by making such a donation we're showing Allah ﷻ that anything and everything we have can be used for Islam and to benefit people, and that no matter what we have, we should always be thinking of how to use it for the pleasure of Allah ﷻ.

To give another example, there was once a very famous companion of the Prophet ﷺ by the name of Salman al-Farsi ﵁. He was originally from Persia and was raised as a fire-worshipper. Salman ﵁ was once sent away on a very important business matter. On his journey, Salman ﵁ saw true Christians praying at a place of worship. Salman ﵁ became very impressed with these people and inquired about their beliefs and, upon his return, told his father that he had found people whose religion was superior to their own. His father became upset and began to worry: he locked Salman ﵁ into a room inside his home. Determined to find the truth, Salman ﵁ heard there was a caravan leaving for the area formerly known as *Sham* – consisting of modern-day Syria and Palestine and their surrounds. Salman ﵁ managed to escape and join the caravan to Sham.

While in Sham, Salman ﵁ searched for the most righteous, knowledgable person of the region. When he was directed to this pious man, a bishop, Salman ﵁ began serving him and studying with him. Over time, Salman ﵁ saw that the bishop was not as pious as people thought. Salman ﵁ stayed with the bishop until he passed away. At that point, the people wanted to prepare a proper burial for him. Salman ﵁ addressed the people and told them that the man whom they had thought was so pious was in fact treacherous. When the people disputed his claim, he told them that he would prove it. He directed the people to a place where the bishop would bury the money he claimed to collect and distribute on behalf of the poor. When they uncovered the hoarded wealth, the people left the body of the bishop unburied and appointed a new bishop to take his place.

Salman ﷺ himself states he had never met someone as pious as this new bishop. Just as he had done with the previous bishop, Salman ﷺ stayed in his service until he reached his deathbed. At that point, Salman ﷺ asked the bishop if there was anyone like him. He was told to go towards Persia and there would be a man on the same path. When Salman ﷺ arrived there, he found another bishop and became his servant. This happened with Salman ﷺ on four separate occasions, where he was directed to find a pious bishop in a different place by a bishop on his deathbed. As a result, he travelled widely in the lands between Syria and Persia. After the final bishop was on his deathbed, Salman ﷺ asked him if there was anyone else with whom he could continue his studies. The bishop informed Salman ﷺ that there were no true Christians left after him. However, he told Salman ﷺ that the time was close for the appearance of the last prophet. He was told to look for the following signs: (1) he will come in a region that has date palm trees growing between mountainous lava rock; (2) he will not eat of food given in charity (sadaqah); (3) he will eat food gifted to him; and (4) he will have the seal of prophethood between his two shoulder blades.

Upon hearing this, Salman ﷺ approached a caravan and sought an agreement with the merchants to take him to such a region as the bishop had described in return for all the wealth he had earnt and saved while serving and studying with the bishops. They agreed, and Salman ﷺ was soon on his way. But when the merchants arrived, they deceived Salman ﷺ and claimed that he was their slave and sold him into slavery. Yet even though Salman ﷺ was now enslaved and moved to another palce, he was content because he was in the region that his teacher had described. Salman ﷺ was then again sold on as a slave, this time to a Jew living in the city of Yathrib (later on the name of Yathrib was changed to *Madinat al-Nabi,* or the City of the Prophet, after the Prophet ﷺ settled there). When he saw Yathrib, he immediately knew that this would be where the final prophet would appear.

Despite the fact that he was enslaved and penniless, Salman ﷺ remained happy as he knew he would reach his desired goal in this city.

Years passed as Salman ﷺ continued to work as a slave. One day, as Salman ﷺ was working, someone approached his Jewish master and gave news of a man claiming to be a prophet, who was of the people of Makkah, and was coming to Yathrib. When Salman ﷺ heard this he almost fell out of the date-palm, as he was harvesting dates. He scurried down and quickly asked the man to repeat himself. Furious at his interjection, Salman's master struck him and told him to get back to work. Thus, Salman ﷺ waited and slowly gathered up a pile of dates. He then took that pile and approached the Prophet ﷺ, presenting it as charity to him and his companions. The Prophet ﷺ replied that he did not eat food given in charity, confirming one of the signs of prophethood that his former teacher had told Salman ﷺ of. On another day, Salman ﷺ returned with another pile of dates, this time presenting it to the Prophet ﷺ and his companions as a gift. The Prophet ﷺ accepted this and ate from it, confirming yet another sign of prophethood.

A short time later, while the Prophet Muhammad ﷺ was seated with his companions waiting for a burial, Salman ﷺ came and began walking around the Prophet ﷺ looking for something. Recognizing what he wanted, the Prophet ﷺ lowered his upper garment, unveiling the seal of prophethood that was between his shoulder blades. At last, the final sign! The long journey of Salman ﷺ had come to the end: he had found the final Prophet ﷺ. His travels in Persia, Syria and Arabia in service of many teachers, his steadfastness in freedom and in slavery, had finally brought him to his desired destination.

Salman ﷺ still remained a slave, but as the Muslims began to participate in various battles and the Prophet ﷺ continued to receive revelation, he wanted, like the companions, to be in close company of the Prophet ﷺ. So he asked the Prophet ﷺ for advice. The Prophet ﷺ advised him to go to his owner and agree to whatever deal was necessary to grant him his freedom. When approached, Salman's owner agreed to free him in return for a large sum of gold and to plant 300 date palm trees and to tend to them until they bore fruit. Salman ﷦ returned in dismay as he felt this would be impossible. The Prophet ﷺ encouraged him to have faith in Allah ﷻ. As they were seated, a companion came to the Prophet ﷺ with a bag of gold in charity. The Prophet ﷺ turned to Salman ﷦ and without looking in the bag told him to take this to his Jewish master, saying that it would be enough. When Salman ﷦ gave it to his master, it was exactly the amount he needed!

Yet the bargain for Salman's freedom was not complete. He still had to plant and tend to the 300 date palms until they bore fruit. In order to help Salman ﷦, the Prophet ﷺ asked his companions to help their brother. They responded by bringing date pits and forming a pile. As soon pile reached 300, the Prophet ﷺ told Salman ﷦ to dig the holes and that he himself would plant the trees. By the blessings that Allah ﷻ placed in the hands of the Prophet ﷺ, all of the 300 trees matured in that same year! So Salman ﷦ gained his freedom and was thereafter always able to be in the company of the Prophet ﷺ.

There were many great things that Salman ﷦ did as a free companion. One of them was his advice that the Muslims dig a trench around Madinah to protect themselves from an army of disbelievers. However, the purpose of this story wasn't to merely tell an amazing tale about a companion of the Prophet ﷺ. Rather, it was to focus your attention on one small point. Imagine if you were a companion and the Prophet ﷺ asked you to help your brother by giving date stones in charity. The companions lived in Madinah, a land filled with dates. Date stones were just as common as pennies are to us now. So, for the companions, putting date stones into a pile was much like us putting pennies in a donation box today. But think of it this way. On the Day of Judgment, each companion who donated a date stone will have shared in the freeing of Salman ﷦. And so any good deed that Salman ﷦ did, a portion of that good deed was shared by each companion that donated to set him free. Now the Hadith quoted earlier, "He from among you who is able to protect himself from the fire should give charity, even if with half a date. If he does not find even that, then with a good word." can be better understood. We should never think that giving a penny won't make a difference. As believers, we never worry about the amount that we are donating; rather, we seek the acceptance of Allah ﷻ for each of our good deeds.

Small deeds can also come in different ways. It is clear that "Every good deed is sadaqah. To meet your brother with a smiling face and to pour out from your bucket into his container are sadaqah." (Hadith) Just smiling at your brother or sister in Islam is considered an act of charity. It amazes us as to how many youth we see who try to act "hard" and never smile. They are costing themselves hundreds of good deeds. One smile, one greeting of *salam* (peace) in the masjid, one kind word can change a person's bad day into a good day and be a means of encouragement for that person to grow closer to Allah ﷻ, as "calling to good is like doing the action." (Hadith) A small piece of advice to or encouragement of our brothers and sisters in Islam can earn us the reward of having actually done the action.

Look at the story of Sultan Muhammad al-Fatih, a ruler of the Ottoman Empire, who studied a Hadith when he was young. The Hadith foretold that a young man would conquer Constantinople and bring Islam to that land. This Hadith impressed Sultan Muhammad so much that he resolved to be that man. Approximately a decade later, Sultan Muhammad led an army of believers over the mountains surrounding the Golden Horn, carrying their boats on their backs and onto the shores surrounding Constantinople. With the city surrounded, the enemy had to give up. We don't know who Sultan Muhammad's teacher of Hadith was, but imagine that just by him teaching this Hadith to Sultan Muhammad and by giving him that encouragement, he too could share in that reward.

It comes clear in narrations that different people did seemingly small and insignificant deeds, but were able to attain heaven through them. There is a clear story about a man who removed an obstacle from a path on a road that Muslims used. For that act, Allah ﷻ gave him Jannah. As a tradition says, "Your smile for your brother is charity. Your removal of stones, thorns, or bones from the paths of people is charity. Your guidance of a person who is lost is charity." (Hadith)

There was another woman who was a prostitute. She was at a well when she found a dog dying of thirst. Out of compassion for that dog, she dipped her shoe into the well and retrieved water for it. In turn, Allah ﷻ forgave her sins, guided her to change her ways, and granted her paradise. These stories are not mentioned just to make us marvel. Rather, they are to remind us that any good deed, no matter how seemingly small it is, may earn us Allah's pleasure and subsequently His paradise.

In the early stage of Islam, the Prophet ﷺ saw a woman leaving Makkah with her belongings. It was uncommon for people at that time to leave their home city unless there was an important reason. Thus, he approached the woman and asked her where she was going. The elderly woman turned to him and said that she was tired of the damage a man by the name of "Muhammad" had done to her community through his preaching of a new religion. She was unaware that the man standing in front of her was that very same man that she was complaining about. Rather than becoming upset, the Prophet ﷺ asked her if he could help her carry her belongings. She agreed and they began walking.

Along the journey the woman continued her complaints about the man named Muhammad. She soon arrived at her destination, and when the Prophet ﷺ placed her belongings on the ground, he asked her if he could settle her into her new home. She agreed and the Prophet Muhammad ﷺ happily worked to set up the place. In all the time he was with her, the Prophet ﷺ addressed her endearingly as "my mother". Once the Prophet ﷺ completed his task, he set to return to Makkah. The elderly woman turned to him and thanked him for his help. She also added that she had not met many people like him, who would volunteer to help her to such a degree, who would only address her as "my mother," and who were willing to accompany her on her move. She asked if, at the very least, he would tell her his name. Very shyly the Prophet ﷺ responded that he was that very same Muhammad that she had been complaining of. This completely shocked the woman, and she turned immediately to the Prophet ﷺ and became a Muslim. She could no longer believe the false claims that had been made against the Prophet ﷺ after she had seen his good character at first hand. These are the effects of doing a good deed that people may otherwise overlook. Sometimes we have people in our community who are ill and we neglect going to visit them.

Allah ﷺ shall say on the Day of Judgment: "O son of man! I was ill and you did not visit me." He will reply: "O my Lord! How could I visit You? You are the Lord of the Worlds!" Allah shall say: "Did you not know that My slave, so-and-so, was ill and you did not visit him? If you had visited him, you would have found Me with him. O son of man! I asked you for food and you did not give it to me." He will reply: "O my Lord! How could I give You food? You are the Lord of the Worlds!" Allah shall say: "Did you not know that My slave, so-and-so, asked you for food and you did not give it to him? Did you not know that if you had given the food, you would have found that with Me? O son of man! I asked you to quench My thirst and you did not." He will say: "O my Lord! How could I quench Your thirst? You are the Lord of the Worlds!" Allah shall say: "My slave, so-and-so, asked you to quench his thirst and you did not. If you had given him to drink, you would have found that with Me." (Hadith)

For some reason, as a community we think of good deeds as only being acts like going to the masjid or fasting or attending a religious lecture. However, great rewards can be attained from actions that are seemingly small. When we see someone stranded on the side of the road and needing help to mend their car, or perhaps seeing an elderly person needing help to carry a heavy bag, we should show kindness and help them, confident in the belief that Allah never neglects to reward a good deed, no matter how small or trivial it may seem to us.

We should also think about the value of teaching others small things. For example, if someone teaches a child Surah al-Fatihah (the first chapter of the Qur'an), then every time that child recites al-Fatihah the teacher will be rewarded. Remember that a person is obliged to recite Surah al-Fatihah seventeen times a day in only the *fard* (mandatory) prayers! If the *Sunnah* (prayers the Prophet ﷺ prayers did with regularity aside from the fard), the *witr* (a prayer prayed after the 'Isha prayer), and any *nafl* (voluntary) prayers, are added then thousands of good deeds in a lifetime await that person who teaches al-Fatihah to another person, an effort of ten minutes. Remember if we teach someone how to perform wudu', then every time that person performs wudu' the teacher is rewarded for it as well. The same rule applies for something as small as teaching someone just to say "salam" or a simple dhikr like "subhanAllah". Everytime that person says these then the teacher receives a similar reward. We should see teaching the basics of religious knowledge as a great opportunity. If there is a child in the neighborhood who needs to learn how to recite the Qur'an, then we should jump at this kind of opportunity. It comes clear in Hadith that every letter a person recites from Qur'an will be rewarded ten times. Now think about what the teacher will receive!

Simply put, we can never underestimate the value of a good deed, and most importantly, we can never underestimate the necessity of doing it regularly. People who work out will say clearly that consistency is the key. Anyone can come in and lift huge amounts of weight once or twice a month, but that will not be beneficial. We see this all the time. A brother will be getting married in a few weeks and he decides that it's time to work out. For the next two weeks he's in the gym working out for hours on end. Yes, he may find some benefit in it. However, people who work out regularly, even if they are unable to lift very much, will find much more benefit in the long run. So, as people who are working on our souls, we need to realize that our good deeds are like our weights. We can do many good deeds on one or two occasions. Yes, we may find some benefit in it, but the reality is that if we did a few good deeds regularly, then we could workout our souls with more proficiency and have more to present to Allah ﷻ on the Day of Judgment.

PRACTICAL SOLUTIONS

- Recite the Qur'an, even if it's only a page or a verse a day.
- Try to give in charity once a week. It would be helpful to tie it into Jumu'ah prayer.
- Recite the du'as the Prophet ﷺ used to read before starting any act.
- Read one hadith a day.
- Make a commitment to follow one Sunnah for the week.
- Identify character faults and make a programme to correct them one by one.
- When we see something wrong we should try to fix it immediately, be it picking up rubbish off the ground or even cheering someone up who is feeling down.
- Try to stay consistent in the amount of worship that you observe.
- Make a habit of thanking Allah ﷻ for all blessings.

See You at the Crossroads
Remembering Death

In life, people are guaranteed many things. Products come with money back guarantees, certain universities or colleges guarantee academic success, and certain advertisements guarantee better looks if we try out their products. But there are no guarantees that we will make a million dollars in our lives, there are no guarantees that we will marry the person we want to marry, and there are no guarantees that we will be the most popular person at school. The only guarantee is that we will die, either sooner or later. It's funny: we focus so much on making money, improving our looks, and doing well at school and work as if that will be what lasts the most. But the only thing that *is* guaranteed, death, is what we try to forget the most. The advice of our Messenger ﷺ was to always remember death. He was very clear when he said, "Make much remembrance of the destroyer of delights." (Hadith)

Nothing can change the mood of any situation like death. When people receive news of a death in the family or of a close friend, irrespective of how great of a day they were having, the reality is that their mood will be altered for a long period of time. We are still shocked and saddened even though death is the only guarantee in this life. People will never be able to predict how much money they will make, what type of homes they will live in, or what cars they will drive. Yet despite the fact we know we are going to die one day, we are very quick to forget this. In fact, it comes in a narration that the Messenger of Allah ﷺ was sitting with his companions when he took a stone and threw it quite some way. He then took a second stone and threw it a shorter distance. Thereafter, he told his companions, indicating the furthest stone, that there lay the hopes and aspirations of humanity, and there, referring to the closer stone, lay death. This beautifully portrays the situation of all human beings. Death brings discomfort to us because we know that it eventually come to us all, but we also carry on with a certain level of denial and prepare only for this world. We can neither escape death nor hide from it.

Wherever you are death will find you, even if you were in high fortified towers. (Qur'an 4:78)

The wise person is the one who recognizes this and subsequently prepares for it. This state is elucidated in a story of the caliph Harun al-Rashid.

Harun al-Rashid was a famous caliph in the Abbasid Empire. He was a righteous man with an appreciation for the arts. One day, while Harun al-Rashid was out of his court, he saw a very pious ascetic by the name of Bahlul Dana. Bahlul was often in such a deep state of remembrance of Allah ﷻ that Harun al-Rashid found his actions to be very strange. As a result, he approached him and addressed him by saying that he had never met an individual as foolish as him. Harun al-Rashid then gave him his staff and said that if he found anyone more foolish than him, that he should then give the staff to that person.

Years passed and Harun al-Rashid eventually became very ill. As a result, Bahlul Dana came to visit him and asked him about his condition. Harun al-Rashid responded by saying that it was clear to him that he would not survive this illness. Bahlul then gave him his staff. Recognizing the staff, Haroon Rasheed asked him why he was giving him back this staff. Bahlul asked Harun al-Rashid as to what he would do anytime he went on a journey. Harun al-Rashid explained that he would send an entourage in advance to the region he was traveling to. That group would prepare his lodgings in order that he would be comfortable upon arrival. They would also take care of any needs that he would have. Upon hearing this, Bahlul asked that if this was the fervor with which he would prepare for a journey in this world then what was the extent of his preparation for the greatest journey he would ever face – the journey from this world back to his Lord. At that moment Harun al-Rashid accepted the staff, realizing he may have been deficient in his preparation for the greatest journey he would ever take.

There are numerous stories about death, but for us it is important that we take the necessary lessons that come with each story. Death has been repeatedly mentioned in both the Qur'an and the Hadith. We know when death is mentioned, our mood changes drastically. Any potential enjoyment we were feeling subsides. The same can occur for people who have experienced the death of a loved one: the thought of death becomes so prevalent in their minds that they abandon sin. If the thought crosses their minds to skip a prayer, the reality of the nearness of death pushes it away. The reason is very simple. Death is the door to the hereafter. Until we cross this threshold, we will never be able to enter into our final abode, either heaven or hell. So remembering death becomes a great tool against Shaytan.

Imagine if Shaytan tries to tempt us towards a sin, and, before we attempt to commit that sin we recall that we may die, there is a great chance that we may not commit that sin. After all, it is very difficult to commit a sin knowing that we may have to return to Allah ﷻ in the state of that sin. This is why many of our great scholars of the past used to dig a grave next to their homes or their beds. On a regular basis, they would lie inside these graves with their eyes closed, imaging death. They would remind themselves that, if they could still open their eyes and climb out, there will come a day when they will remain in their graves and their loved ones will cover them in dirt. And then they will have to experience either the pleasures or the punishments of the grave.

There are many narrations that describe the moments of death. These narrations really aid a person in understanding that death is a very severe event. In fact, Imam Qurtubi 🪷 writes that on one occasion Prophet Ibrahim ﷺ was speaking to the Angel of Death when he asked the angel to reveal how he appears to a righteous person at the time of death. The Angel of Death asked Prophet Ibrahim ﷺ to turn away, which he did. When he turned back and saw the Angel of Death, he exclaimed that if that were the only reward that a believer received at the time of death, it would be sufficient. Prophet Ibrahim ﷺ then asked the Angel of Death how he would appear to a sinner. The Angel of Death refused, but when Prophet Ibrahim ﷺ persisted, the Angel of Death asked him to turn away. When he turned back again he saw the Angel of Death in such a terrifying form that he immediately fainted. When he became conscious again, he stated that if a sinner received no punishment other than seeing the Angel of Death in that terrible form, it would be sufficient. Imagine how grotesque and frightening that form must be that on top of the torments of hell that await the sinful.

Other narrations also state the manner in which people pass away depends on what their deeds were like. For example, the Angel of Death approaches the good soul and draws it out gently, like water trickling from a fountain. However, for the sinful and disobedient soul, the Angel of Death, coming in a terrible appearance, will tear out the soul. The soul will try to take refuge and hide within the body, but the Angel will not let it escape. It comes in Hadith that extracting the disbelieving soul will be like tearing wet wool caught around a thorny branch. These images have been given in Hadith in order for us to recall them and so be aware of the seriousness of death and the need to remember it in order to save ourselves from the first stages of punishment.

Furthermore, the remembrance of death itself carries other benefits. On one occasion, the Prophet ﷺ was with his companions and likened the heart to iron, in that it is capable of rusting.

> **Verily, without doubt a stain grows upon the heart from what they did.** (Qur'an 83:15)

The companions immediately asked the Messenger of Allah ﷺ how they could remove that rust. The Prophet ﷺ told them that reciting the Qur'an and remembering death were means to remove that rust. This may not seem like a big deal, but as we mentioned earlier, the heart becomes covered with a seal by the sins of an individual. Eventually, if a person neither stops sinning nor removes that rust, the heart becomes completely encrusted by that rust, or sealed.

Allah has put a seal on their hearts (Qur'an 2:7)

This seal leads the spiritual compass of a person to go awry. Sinning becomes easy until the person eventually drowns in sin and is no longer capable of getting out of that state. Then, after death,

For them is a great punishment. (Qur'an 2:7)

The Prophet ﷺ mentioned that "Death is a gift for a believer." (Hadith) This Hadith is fascinating because most people hate death and have an aversion to it. But, the reality for the believers is that this world is merely a bus stop. Some people will get on an earlier bus, while others get on a later bus. However, eventually everyone gets on board their bus and goes to their destination.

Every soul shall taste death. (Qur'an 3:185)

The same applies to this world. Some people will leave this world earlier, while others leave later. However, everyone must leave this world and go to their destination eventually. And the bus that every person must board is death. For the believer, the destination is to be desired. We know that heaven awaits those who have spent their nights and days for the sake of Allah ﷺ.

Indeed those who believe and do good deeds for them is a feast in the gardens of paradise. They will live therein forever, and they will not wish for any change. (Qur'an 18:107-108)

So, for us, death is something that we welcome. It is through that gate that we will attain the Jannah that has been promised to us. But the only way we can welcome death is by remembering it constantly.

PRACTICAL SOLUTIONS

- Take a moment of the day to remember what our final destination will be.
- Try to attend a funeral (*janazah*) prayer whenever possible.
- Try to visit the cemetary at least once every month.
- When praying, consider that it might be your last one.
- Supplicate to Allah ﷻ that our last words be the best of words, the declaration of faith (*shahadah*).
- Supplicate that the last of our actions be the best of our actions.
- Supplicate that Allah ﷻ protects you from the punishment of the grave.
- Supplicate that Allah ﷻ protects you from the punishment of the hereafter.
- Supplicate that Allah ﷻ helps you to answer correctly the questions in the grave.
- Supplicate for all those who have passed away.
- Visit the sick.
- Volunteer in a nursing home or a hospital ward.
- Try to participate in washing a dead body prior to its burial.

Closing Time
Epilogue

Living in places that are not predominantly Muslim can be tough. However, we also have to recognize what a great blessing this is from Allah ﷻ. The religious freedom that we find is not readily available even in some Muslim countries. Although Islam may be the official religion, certain ideologies of Islam have become dominant and others are not allowed to be practised openly. In our countries we are free to openly practice the Sunnah, pray in masajid, and have differences of opinion. There are many great elements of our lands that we often overlook and we can fall into the trap of being ungrateful. The idea isn't for us to become hermits who hide away, isolating ourselves from the rest of society. This was never the way of the Prophet ﷺ, and his example is the best example. Rather, he was involved in his community and would be readily available to help anyone who was in need.

In fact, it comes very clear in Hadith that the Prophet ﷺ himself spoke about a covenant that he made in the time of *jahilliyah* (a term referring to an age of "ignorance" in pre-Islamic Arabia) that if it had been presented to him during the time of Islam, he would still have participated in it. It was his constant interaction with his neighbours, both Muslims and non-Muslims that enabled him to spread the light of Islam. On the occasion in which the Prophet ﷺ first called his close family and tribesmen to the mountain, he questioned whether or not they would believe him if he warned them of an army on the other side of the mountain that was ready to attack them.

They stated that they would in fact believe him. We have to ask ourselves how this group was so quick to believe the Prophet ﷺ. The reason was, as they stated, he had proven himself as being *as-Sadiq* (trustworthy) and *al-Amin* (truthful).

On another occasion, there was a malicious Jewish neighbours of the Prophet ﷺ who would constantly lay garbage in his path, intending for the clothes and body of the Prophet ﷺ to be sullied. One day, when the Prophet ﷺ went out, he did not find his path covered in garbage. As a result, he enquired as to whether everything was OK with his Jewish neighbour, and discovered that his neighbour's son was very ill. The Prophet ﷺ immediately rushed to his home to visit his son. Imagine how the Jewish man must have felt when he saw his enemy visiting to enquire after the well-being of his child. The Prophet ﷺ saw that the child was extremely ill and was going to pass away. As a result, he turned to the young boy and advised him to become Muslim. The young boy turned to his father for advice. The father, overwhelmed by the character and kindness of the Prophet ﷺ, told his son to do as he said. The boy took shahadah and passed away as a Muslim. These incidents were not isolated. There are countless examples like this from the Sunnah. It inevitably comes to the fact that the Prophet ﷺ was involved in his community and did not shun them.

The purpose of our book was to make us understand that there will be some pitfalls and temptations within our societies. However, we cannot shun society itself. There are many good people who live amongst us, from whom we can benefit. We know that 'Umar ؓ had a servant who was not Muslim. The character of this servant was so exemplary that 'Umar ؓ wanted to make him a governor of one of the Islamic provinces. When 'Umar ؓ asked him to become Muslim and accept this position, the man replied that he wasn't interested in changing his religion. 'Umar ؓ did not become upset. He saw the goodliness of this man and benefited from him, just as his servant benefited from the various great characteristics of 'Umar ؓ. This is how we need to be as well. The Prophet ﷺ himself said, "The creation is a family of Allah. And the most beloved of creation to Allah are the ones who are the most beneficial to His creation." (Hadith) It is not possible to be of general benefit to all of creation if we Muslims only keep amongst ourselves. There are treasures that everyone carries within them for "wisdom is the lost treasure of the believer." (Hadith)

The Hadith clearly states that there will be ways through which we can benefit from our neighbors. It is important for us to recognize these treasures and work together to bring a state of peace upon this Earth. When Muslims conquered foreign lands, they brought to the people of that land a guarantee that they will be protected, despite their religious beliefs. To the extent that on one occasion, when the Muslims were threatened by an army that they were not sure they would be victorious against, they turned to the non-Muslims of their land and returned the *jizyah* (tax taken from non-Muslims in return for security and protection by the Muslim army). When asked why they had done this, the leaders of the Muslims said that this money was taken to guarantee protection against the enemies. Since they were unable to give that guarantee in this particular battle, they felt returning this money was the only way to remain just.

Life will be tough, and all of us will have difficulties. We have to realize that our Islam is to be practiced in the midst of these difficulties and through our patience and struggle, Allah ﷻ will reward us for our intentions and actions.

We began working on this book three years ago with the intention of producing a forty-page booklet on ways to identify Shaytan's deceptions and how to protect ourselves from them. Now, three years later, by the grace and mercy of Allah ﷻ, we have completed this book. If there are any errors or you have any suggestions to improve the book, please feel free to contact the publishers or to contact us directly by email: habeebq@yahoo.com and saad.quadri@gmail.com. We ask that you pray for this and future projects. We seek to gain Allah's pleasure by means of this work in hopes of meeting with you all, dear readers, in the highest level of Jannah.

And their greeting therein (in Heaven) *will be peace. And the last of their calling is "All praise be to Allah, Lord of the worlds."* (Qur'an 10:10)

Acknowledgements
Thank You

First and foremost we want to begin by thanking Allah ﷻ for giving us the opportunity to serve Him and His din through this book. It is only through His *tawfiq* (guidance) that we were able to complete this task. We also want to thank and send peace and blessings upon the Prophet ﷺ, who truly has been and always will be our guiding light in dark times.

We want to also thank our wives, Aisha Siddiqui and Sana Mohiuddin, and our children for their unrelenting support and patience through the many ups and downs that came with writing this book. Without their understanding and patience, particularly regarding our insane schedules, this book would not be in your hands today.

Many people have been involved in reading through and editing our work, giving suggestions and criticisms along the way: Fawzia Ahmed, Khadijah Ahmed, Jill Alali, Nassir Kotelensky, Kazim Mohammad, Sue Labadi, Fatima Quadri, Saba Quadri, Zarina Tawakul, and Azhar Usman.

There were many other people who were indirectly involved in helping this book come to completion like our parents who believed in us and regularly showed us the correct path by deed and word. We also want to thank our siblings and friends, from whose watchful eyes we could never escape, and who provided us with the good company we so direly needed. We want to thank our family, especially our aunts and uncles, who are our second parents, and our cousins who were like brothers and sisters to us.

We would like to especially thank our teachers and mentors who took time out to mould our delicate minds and hearts. Truly the inheritors of the prophets are constantly sought after for their wealth and for them to give of their wealth to paupers like us was the height of human generosity.

We especially want to thank all of the youth we have met in our travels and work. Some of you we have only met once, while others we have seen more of. You may not know it, but you all have helped us along the way.

Finally, we would like to thank all of the Islamic organizations that we have or have not been a part of. It is caring people like you whose time and effort helps to keep the *ummah* (Muslim community) moving forward.

About the Authors

Habeeb Quadri is Principal of the MCC Full Time School in Morton Grove, Illinois. He has a Bachelors in Teaching of History and a Masters in School Administration. He is currently taking courses at the Harvard University Graduate School of Education's Principal's Center, where he has accumulated over 150 clock hours of instruction. In addition to his teaching and administrative experience in public and private schools, Habeeb has delivered hundreds of lectures throughout the United States, Canada, and abroad, on Islam, society, and social problems confronting Muslim youth and the community at large for the last 15 years. Additionally, Habeeb maintains an active interest in educational consulting. He has started his own educational consulting company called High Quality Educational Consulting in which he has partnered with the IQRA International Educational Foundation as a consultant. Habeeb has conducted workshops for weekend and full-time Islamic schools, public schools, and universities around the world, delivering presentations on such topics as classroom management, motivational techniques for students and faculty, curriculum development, Muslim sensitivity training, and overall educational administration. He was the religious and cultural consultant for the children's book *Under the Ramadan Moon* by Sylvia Whitman. Habeeb has also written *Thank God It's Jumu'ah* and *The Best of the Best: Sayings from our Beloved* and is currently working on two projects regarding parental advice on dealing with Muslim youth and a children's story book.

Sa'ad Quadri was born and raised in the Chicagoland area. Having spent his entire youth studying in public schools, Sa'ad completed high school a year early in order to pursue studies in the Islamic sciences at the Institute of Islamic Education (IIE). He spent three years there memorizing the Qur'an, studying Arabic, and learning the basic principles of deen. Thereafter he attended Northern Illinois University (NIU) where he majored in English and minored in History, and he is pursuing his Masters in Education at DePaul University. Currently, Sa'ad is continuing his Islamic studies in the Sacred Learning Individual Study Program. By profession, Sa'ad is a teacher and dean at the College Preparatory School of America (CPSA), located in Lombard, Illinois.

Appendix

	Each day in America among all children
1	mother dies in childbirth.
4	children are killed by abuse or neglect.
5	children or teens commit suicide.
8	children or teens are killed by firearms.
76	babies die before their first birthdays.
182	children are arrested for violent crimes.
366	children are arrested for drug abuse.
390	babies are born to mothers who received late or no prenatal care.
860	babies are born at low birthweight.
1,186	babies are born to teen mothers.
1,707	babies are born without health insurance.
1,887	public school students are corporally punished.
2,171	babies are born into poverty.
2,539	high school students drop out.
2,341	babies are born to mothers who are not high school graduates.
2,455	children are confirmed as abused or neglected.
2,539	high school students drop out.
3,742	babies are born to unmarried mothers.
4,440	children are arrested.
17,072	public school students are suspended.